Live Greater

Think Deeper

Love Better

SPIRITUAL REFLECTIONS
FOR THE HEART, MIND, & SOUL

LIVE IN LOVE PUBLISHING

Live in Love Publishing

Copyright © 2019 by BaSean A. Jackson

ISBN: 978-0-578-43925-9

Cover Design/Book Design by Cameia Williams

Printed in the U.S.A.

Wow!!! That is the first word that comes to mind as I read Live Greater, Think Deeper, Love Better. The enthusiastic zeal and zest that the writer has for God's people and life is evident in every reflection.

— *Dr. Carolyn Ann Knight*

He creatively weaves through these poles in creative and imaginative connections. This is a read which will surprise many.

— *Rev. Dr. Randall C. Bailey,*
Distinguished Prof. of Hebrew Bible, Emeritus, Interdenominational
Theological Center, Atlanta, GA

In reading his book I am reminded of the power of love and the importance of deep reflection and how that can improve the quality of one's life and one's community.

— *Dr. Joseph Barrow*
Superintendent of Fayette County Schools

He has a unique and captivating gift to make preaching relevant, real, and relational. In a time such as this, there is a great need to share the Word of God in visionary and inviting ways.

— *Rev. Edward Johnson, Pastor*
Flat Rock AME Church, Fayetteville, Georgia
Mayor, City of Fayetteville, Georgia

A blessing is not a blessing unless you can give it away and these messages are something that you not only can give away, but you want to share them with others.

— *Chuck Hardon*
Co-Founder of the PoWEr Builders Movement

Rev. Jackson has written a powerfully inspiring book that will change lives and strengthen communities. He writes with the love ethic of bell hooks and offers a theologically grounded roadmap for individuals and communities seeking to live lives of faith and integrity.

— *Bernard "Chris" Dorsey, President of Disciples Higher Education and Leadership Ministries*

As I read Live Greater, Think Deeper, Love Better: Spiritual reflections for the heart, mind, and soul, I smiled often ... with B.A. leveraging a clever style of engaging the reader with thought provoking premises intertwined with questions and examples ultimately leading to a better understanding and application within one's life ... This book is filled with nuggets of wisdom and challenges the reader along the way with suggestions to activate our desired behaviors and practices. Simple but complex. Eloquent but candid. Light-hearted but serious. B.A. takes us on a journey via an allegory of life and love and trial and triumph and invites us to seek a better personal understanding of how to be our best self.

— *Marcus G. Glover*
Executive - Hospitality and Lodging Industry

His messages of hope are powerful instruments delivered with such clarity that our beliefs are challenged, and dedication renewed. ... The beauty of the narrative is that we can reflect on the examples and apply the takeaways that best fit our personal situation. Whether it's the Apostle Paul's work ethic or the rapper Lil Wayne's longevity in the Hip Hop world the tests of how to become better fruit are plainly stated. However, B.A. Jackson also challenges us as Christians to reevaluate how the church addresses topics such as Same Sex Marriage and Prosperity vs. Poverty that is illuminated in a way that bears reflection and demands action.

— *Steven L. Reed*
Probate Judge Montgomery County, Alabama

From Lil' Wayne to his little boy, B.A. Jackson shows us that the little moments in our culture, in our news headlines and in our lives can teach us how to grow in our faith. His reflections encourage us to follow Jesus by loving God, loving ourselves and loving our neighbor—even the ones we disagree with—in thought-provoking and creative ways.

— *Dr. Beth Corrie*
Associate Professor in the Practice of Youth Education
and Peacebuilding Candler School of Theology

B.A. Jackson brilliantly takes readers through a simple yet provocative path of storytelling, sharing, and learnings that center Love as the answer to today's most complex problems. What I love most about this book, is that it goes beyond teaching the reader how to improve themselves, but it implores today's Christians to make society better by centering solutions to problems in Love, not age old tradition. As the former National Criminal Justice Director of NAACP and current Vice President of a leading national justice reform organization, this book will be my go-to for breaking down complicated issues and inspiring people to get involved in activism, love-centered activism.

— *Robert Rooks, Co-founder and Vice President*
Alliance for Safety and Justice

This book is dedicated to Patricia and Bryce.
No two people have ever moved me more.

Acknowledgements

This book is written with immeasurable and ineffable gratitude. I want to thank Patricia Perry who is forever my example of how to be great at life and in life. You have been God's greatest human demonstration of grace and Love to me. No one knows me as well as you do, and this means no one has really Loved me as much as you have. So much of who I am and what I do is due to your Love and presence in my life making me better. More to the point, you have made my life greater, you have made me think deeper, and you give me a paradigm of Loving better.

I want to thank the greatest inspiration of my life, my son Bryce Austin Jackson. I learn so much about Love through being your father. I have been so blessed by your presence, courage, humor, intellect, and zest for life. When my life is at its darkest, you are my brightest spot, and when times have been at their worst, you have been what is best. You have literally saved my life. I pray someday I can repay you for that and for all the lessons you teawch me in my attempts to be an apt father.

I am grateful to my mother and father. My mother is the greatest example of commitment to God and the Christian life that I have ever witnessed amongst my inner circle. Thank you for Loving me, pushing me, disciplining me, lecturing me, helping me, and comforting me. I even Love our theological debates. There is no Love like a mother's Love and you have made this cliché come to life for me. I am also forever grateful for my dad. My "Daddy" is the foundation of who I am as a minister. I grew up seeing him go to sleep at night and wake up almost every morning with a book in his hand. He taught me my first preaching class. He was the first person to show me the value of study and be an example of Christian conviction. No matter what,

Acknowledgements

I am grateful for what God has done for me, through you. My parents are also responsible for my two younger siblings, Britney and Banikah. I am grateful to have lived long enough to go from changing your diapers and combing your hair to getting lectures, help, and support from you. Britney, thank you for letting me share a piece of your story in this book. Banikah, thank you for being the closest thing to an older baby sister a person can be. I Love both of you.

There is no other person, outside of me, more responsible for this book than Kendra Shipmon. Thank you for pushing me to make these thoughts into one comprehensive text and for staying on top of me by giving me deadlines to break. Thank you for sitting and working with me when I was too sad, hurt, or stuck to move myself by myself. Your passion is to help people be their best selves. So, in some ways you owe me because as long as I am alive and not living up to my best, I will keep you in business. Your purpose and passion make me better and I am grateful.

There are friends too many to name who continue to serve as my Love community. I roll in packs. So to the SSCrew, The Bears, The Circle, preacher friends, my kickball team, and my spiritual group communities thank you for making me laugh, helping me to have fun, and holding me accountable for being better. In all of these groups you allow me to be my uncut and unfiltered self and I will forever be grateful for having places and people who see me as friend, teammate, and brother.

Thank you to Fellowship of Love Church. I continue to be thrilled that we can tackle the possibility of revolutionizing the idea and the impact of church. We have not the time for me to detail all the ways I have experienced you Loving me and Loving each other. I have learned so much from our meetings, worship experiences, events, talks in the parking lot, and conversations on the phone. I am also happy to work with a staff that learns, Loves, and has fun together. All of those I have worked with past and present have helped me grow. So thank you to Janace Coleman, John Clemons, Delesslyn Kennebrew, Candice Austin, Shanika Perry, Allison Henderson-Brooks, James Dorsey, Candle Lockett, Darlene Byrd, Brandon Perkins, and Sarah Perkins. Finally, to my two soul brothers in life and in music, Jason Sylvain and Dell Phillips; we came together when FOLC was just an idea and over ten years, six musical CD's, 50+ songs, and more than 500 worship experiences together we are still sharing "highs and lows." Thank you!

Finally, thanks to the team of people who have helped in other ways with this book. Thank you to Kassia Walker who is the closest thing I have to a personal editor. Thank you to Dawn Oparah and Ogechi Oparah for your brilliance, Love, and abundant support of me. A huge grateful shout out to my favorite graphic artist, Cameia Williams. You are the architect of the visual Fellowship of Love Church Brand and you are amazing.

Contents

Think Deeper

Contents

#LiveThinkLove

Introduction

If the man I was in my twenties would have had his way I would have never written this book. In fact, I would have never been a pastor. In those days, I was convinced that my life and my lifestyle was not built for church. Believe me, it wasn't! Yet, it was more than just about who I was, it was also about what I experienced Christianity to be through the church. I grew up a conservative Christian in Texas. I was taught the fundamental views that most Baptist Christians in conservative churches are taught. We are right, and everyone else is wrong. The Bible is the perfect, inerrant, and accurate Word of God spoken directly from God to the authors. Jesus is the only way to God and to heaven. Questioning these truths, and many others, was not just a matter of being right or wrong, it was a matter of being eternally damned or living forever. As I studied religion and philosophy at Morehouse College and went to get my Master of Divinity at the Interdenominational Theological Center, for the first time I encountered the act of critically thinking about my beliefs.

In my experience, church was not the place for thinking. Maybe that's too strong. You could think, as long as your thoughts took you to the answers you had been taught all along. However, as I began living on my own, I also began thinking on my own. Through my encounters with authors (dead and alive), professors, and classmates, I began to rethink my spirituality, theology, and beliefs. I also, for various reasons, became disenchanted with the church and church people. I had decided I would never pastor. The church was too narrow, too judgmental, and too mean for me to want to lead one. I wanted to be free to struggle with and even challenge the Bible, and I wanted to be free to hear from God through life as I lived it.

Introduction

Clearly, some things have changed. I not only pastor a church, I founded one. What has not changed is my commitment to thinking. Thinking is one of my deepest Loves. Live Greater, Think Deeper, Love Better is a book that is born out of a complex mingling of my lived experiences, my Christian commitments, my engagement with scripture and theology, and my critical reflections. Yet all of these are constantly filtered through my prioritization and prizing the virtue of Love. Like me, this book is not very holy, but it is deeply spiritual. By holy, I mean that stiff, pietistic, too heavenly bound to be any earthly good, over-spiritualized version of Christianity that I find mostly unattractive. I value the Bible, but I do not beat people over the head with it. I do not understand my choice to be Christian as one that allows me to have a monopoly on God or ideas about God. I strive to be convicted without being dogmatic.

In life, I like to have fun, experience spiritual and secular things, and I Love to laugh. Throughout this book, you will experience my humor or at least my attempts at humor. You will also get to meet my son Bryce. My friends often thank God for Bryce because they fear without him I would have little to preach about. This may be true. I talk about my son a lot. God has spoken and revealed more to me through fatherhood than in any other aspect of my life. Growing, parenting, nurturing, failing, and observing Bryce is one of my greatest joys and largest sources of inspiration.

In the reflections written in this book you will experience my spirituality at work. It is a spirituality that finds answers in the everyday happenings of life. It is a spirituality that struggles to think about the world as we find it and as we try to change it. It is a spirituality deeply shaped by the ultimate value of Love that I have learned through Christ.

Whatever spirituality does it ought to help us to learn how to live. Spirituality is a part of every arena of life and should speak pointedly, even if not always clearly, to all that we do. Spirituality cannot just be about heaven, and it should not just be about holiness. Yet this was the overwhelming feeling I received growing up as a Christian. I experienced much of the Christianity of my childhood as a challenge to be holy in the midst of a world of temptation. Be holy .... get to heaven. Be holy .... get to heaven. This was the essence of the Christianity of my youth. Three major things changed and expanded my understanding of Christianity and my practice of spirituality. I lived more. I thought more. I learned and experienced Love more.

I believe in every arena of human existence we find ourselves asking and answering the Love question. In our romantic lives, we are searching for the best ways to express and experience Love. At our theological best, we search to understand God and God's Love and ask what this means for how we will live and Love. Even in our politics, when we determine what rules will govern our communal living, we are essentially asking how will we Love each other appropriately so that we can have the opportunity to live and thrive. Love finds itself in every corner of human existence. This is why the reflections in these pages touch so many aspects of life and experience. I do not talk about romantic Love specifically all that much. Maybe at this point in my life I need to do more reading than writing on this topic. Yet, there is so much in these reflections that I believe will make us better romantic partners. More importantly, I believe looking at Love beyond romance helps us become better humans.

In many ways, this book is about doing the work of Love. Since Love at its best is lived and not just felt, to work for a better life is to do the work of Love. It is almost impossible to Love well without working hard. I know we would rather have a more fantastical view of Love. We wish Love could just happen, last forever, and be eternally filled with bliss. But the truth is in every arena of Love—romantic, spiritual, relational, political and even self-Love—we have to work at it to be good. This may be why so many of us fall short when it comes to Love. When we are faced with the unsettling reality that Love does not exist in life like it does in fairy tales, disenchantment turns into disappointment and disappointment turns into despair. It is hard to Love well from a place of despair. Desperate lives search for what is easy. This is so obvious in romance and with how we choose to exist in the world. It is sometimes easier to stay in a toxic relationship that is comfortable than struggle through the discomfort of loneliness and figure out what self-Love really means. It is sometimes easier to move to another relationship than it is to struggle to really know someone and be known. It is easier to live in bias and stereotype than try to understand another person or people. It is easier to be provincial than it is to be complex. It is easier to exclude than it is to include. It is easier to live in a world of clear-cut superior and inferior people than to ask how difference means different and not better. Love is not easy. Many of the reflections in this book push us to ask ourselves how we can Love ourselves and others when it is does not come easy.

My prayer is that this book inspires you, challenges you, comforts you, and provokes you to think. I hope you will not always agree with me. I remind my church family all the time, it is not my job to tell you how to think. However, it is my job to provoke thinking. If this book at any point helps your life, stirs a thought, or helps you to Love in a more substantial way, I feel sufficiently used by God. I hope some of the pages here will cause great conversation. I hope something you read will help you to Live Greater, Think Deeper, and Love Better.

We can be successful and never be great, but we can never be great and not be successful. I first heard the distinction between success and greatness through one of my intellectual heroes Dr. Cornel West. In his grandiloquent and preacher-esque style (you have to use big words when talking about Dr. West), he suggested that success is a different project than greatness. Success is what most Americans are born and bred to Love, live, and die trying to achieve. Success is usually tied to some sort of accumulation whether it be money, awards, titles, or some combination of these and others. Success is almost always measured by what we accumulate. Success in sports in measured by how many victories, yards, points, hits, and goals one obtains. Success in business is usually measured by how much money one earns, how much market share one claims, or how many stores one opens. Even in church, success is often measured amongst pastors and parishioners by how many members one claims or how much money one accrues. Greatness is different.

If success is measured by what we receive from the world, greatness is measured by what we give to the world. Greatness is not just about our ability to consume. It is about our ability to contribute. If we have mountains of success, but don't make a molehill's worth of difference in the world, we have missed the point. Even contemporary Christianity teaches us that God's best virtue is the ability to be a means to our individual success. God's selling points are the wealth God can give us, the success God can help us achieve, and the peace and happiness God can provide us. I too believe that an intentional and consistent relationship with God is able to afford us these things. I just don't believe that these things are all that our spirituality ought to bring into existence. If we are sold on God based on the desire for personal success, then each of us becomes the point of our spiritual being in the world. Success theology can make God only relevant to "our" personal wants, without ever making our life and purpose relevant to God's divine will. It's not that success is "bad." It is just dangerous if that is all there is to the purpose of our life. I believe there is more. I am convinced that all of us are created to be great, because we are all created to make an indelible imprint on the world.

Our world suffers from a lack of greatness. And by greatness I mean, great people and people striving to be great. Our lives are not only greater with God, but our living can also be great if we take God seriously. These next few pages are not just about you and your salvation and success. They are about how our personal spirituality, intentionality, and improvement can help bring about the salvation of the world. Oh, I want you to be successful. I just don't want you to only be successful. Your success should ultimately culminate in your being great.

1

Start Right to Avoid Ending Wrong

Christmas is one of my favorite holidays of the year. I Love family, I Love the food, but most of all I Love the anticipation and excitement of gift giving to those I Love the most. From the pre-Christmas list negotiations to the post-Christmas observations, there is nothing more fulfilling than Christmas with Bryce.

Like many parents my post-Christmas plans always include putting together Christmas gifts. One particular Christmas, I remember Bryce begging for a mini-motorcycle/dirt bike as early as the summer. Of course I adamantly refused, and of course by the time Christmas came …. I caved. Bryce was ecstatic and excited to receive the gift and just as eager to put it together so that he could ride it. In his haste and enthusiasm to get on his bike, Bryce decided that he would help put it together and begin without me. He looked at the first thing that he thought made sense and began snapping, connecting, and putting things together. I finally got to the bike, read the instructions, and realized we had a major problem. The work Bryce had done to put the bike together had actually kept us from putting the bike together. We were at an impasse. It was not because we lacked the desire to have a complete bike. It was not because we were unwilling to do the work of putting the bike together. It was not because we were without the tools to put the bike together. We were unable to complete the bike because we started putting it together at the wrong place. Eventually, we had to undo what Bryce had done and begin at step 1, where the instructions told us to begin.

Whether it's on Mondays, your birthday, the new year, or when you bought this book, we often find ourselves trying to start over. Many of us make goals, resolutions, commitments, and promises in an attempt to put our lives back together, fix our lives, and/or make our lives complete. Nevertheless, if you are anything like me you often find yourself eventually frustrated, exhausted, and or unhappy with the results. Some of us feel like we are stuck and at an improvement impasse, unable to move any higher, go any further, or progress to any place in life that is better. I want to suggest that some of our inabilities to reach our goals, fulfill our dreams, or carry our ambitions, are not because of a lack of desire. It is not because we are unwilling to put in the work. It is not because we do not have the tools that we need to be our best and perform at our most optimal. It simply may be because we are starting in the wrong place.

This time, I want to encourage you to start with your SPIRIT! I am convinced that spiritual health, spiritual discipline, and spiritual work is the foundation for each and every other part of our lives, goals, and ambitions coming together. The Apostle Paul is attributed to have written to a young, up and coming Timothy, and he writes to him and gives him these words of advice: "Do not neglect the spiritual gift within you." I believe this is so relevant to those of us who have determined that "this time" will be better than the last time or that this week will be better than next week. More importantly, to those of us who have decided that we will be better in our future than we were in our past, I believe our best chance is to begin with our spiritual growth. So, as you commit to eating better, improving your finances, starting your business, going back to school, bettering your relationship, making a bigger impact, cooking more, spending less money, just reading this book; all of these will be more achievable if you can become a stronger spiritual being. Your life can be fixed, your situation can improve, and you can be complete, but you have to start at the right place.

Take Action

As you begin this book, start a spiritual practice for a set amount of time. Examples may be fasting for seven days, having a 30-day prayer journey, or 40 days of meditation. This is your spiritual journey. You decide the practice and you decide the time. The important thing is to be intentional about your spirit.

2

Stick Your Neck Out

"Behold the turtle: he only makes progress when he sticks his neck out."
- James Bryant Conant

The other day as I was reading, I came across this quote that stopped me in my tracks. Immediately, my sermonic antennae went up and my theological telescope took focus. James Conant (1893-1978), former president of Harvard University, brings us this metaphor that may help us make the next move and take the next step in our lives. Have you ever considered the turtle? It is a reptile most popularly known for its slow movement and its impregnable natural defense mechanism. I can remember growing up marveling at a turtle's ability to retreat into its shell and become unassailable even to the likes of animals ten times its size. However, Conant's simple observation reminds us that one of the turtle's greatest capacities can become its primary constraint. Its most pronounced strength can also be its most prominent weakness. If the turtle simply wants to protect itself, it will be fine living life in its shell. Yet, at some point, the turtle has to move, thrive, and make progress. Interestingly enough, in order to eat, move, and swim, a turtle has to give up its safety and take a risk. A turtle cannot live, simply protecting itself. If it is to do anything of significance it must stick its neck out.

Such is the case with our lives. Too often, we can find ourselves living our lives simply attempting to keep ourselves from hurt, harm, and danger. We make decisions seeking to avoid rejection, elude failure, and escape defeat. We can successfully protect ourselves from these things by staying in our shell. If being protected is our chief aim, then going into a shell works. However, at some point we realize that life cannot be lived and nothing meaningful can happen without progress. To exist, we sometimes have to protect ourselves, but to really live, we have to make progress; and to make progress, we have to risk sticking our neck out. Often, the amount of progress we want to make is connected to the amount of risk we are willing to take.

Jesus tells a story about this called the parable of the talents. In this story, a man gives three people large but different sums of money. Two of them double their money and one goes and hides the money given out of fear. After some time the man comes back and asks the people to give an account of their handling of the money. Upon hearing that the first two have doubled their money, he rewards them. However, when he hears that one essentially went into a shell and hid the money out of fear, he takes the money back. Amongst other things, Jesus' parable, just like James Conant's reminder both speak to our willingness to take risks. More importantly, they both speak to the profound importance of progress. God has not called us to live our lives prioritizing protection over progress. In our relationships, careers, finances, and even in our spirituality, too many times we make decisions with protection in mind. However, today is a good day to choose progress. Life is waiting to be lived, goals are waiting to be achieved, dreams are waiting to be fulfilled, and progress is waiting to be gained. Still, the next step, the next level, the next gain, or the next accomplishment will not happen, until you come out of your shell and stick your neck out.

Take Action

Make a list of actions that are risky, but also carry the promise of progress. Choose one thing from that list and try it. Push yourself to attempt as much of the list as possible.

3

You Don't Have a Backup

Tom Brady is the most decorated and arguably the greatest quarterback in the history of the National Football League. He has played in eight Super Bowls and won five. In his fifth Super Bowl victory, he won in a dazzling fashion as he came back from a 25-point deficit to win in overtime. I hated it! I am not a Patriots or a Tom Brady fan, but I do recognize that he has a great biographical story and a stellar football resume. He was a 6th round pick in the draft and pretty much discarded as being too slow, too unathletic, and too weak to be a good quarterback in the NFL. In fact, Tom Brady started as a backup quarterback to Drew Bledsoe. He has gone from backup to arguably the greatest quarterback to ever play the game. By stepping in for Bledsoe years ago, Brady has ushered in an era of Patriot greatness that is really unrivaled in NFL history. Have I told you that I hate it?

However, Tom Brady's story reminds me of how important backups are in sports. I learned this firsthand years ago when I played football and was on a team that had been so decimated by injuries that one of our positions was down to its last possible player. I can remember the coach urgently yelling at this player as he ran on the field, "You don't have a backup!" I can also remember the panic that came over us as teammates as we realized that whatever was going to be done at that position, only one person could do it. I remember thinking that if he got hurt, we would have a void on our team and on the field that would most likely cripple our chances of winning that day. Finally, I remember the terrifying, yet awesome reality of what it must feel like to be the only person that can do what you do.

In some sense, this is the reality of each and every one of our lives. Scripture reminds us that we are "fearfully and wonderfully made" (Psalms 139:14). Just like we each have an inimitable fingerprint, we also have a purpose for our lives that we are uniquely created to perform. Our lives, experiences, situations, families, friends, and mentors uniquely shape and mold us such that we are fitted to fulfill a Divine purpose. We have been created and preserved to get on the field and do something only we can do. And we do not have backups! When we choose to live beneath our potential and below our purpose, we leave an eternal void in the world that no one can fill quite like us.

I want to remind you today that you do not have a backup. Your life is profoundly meaningful and unique, and we ought to live everyday with the urgency of a person who could rob the world of the blessing that is your purpose. Your call cannot be answered by anyone but you. Your position cannot be played by anyone but you. Without your contribution, the world loses something it can never get back. So, move into the rest of your life knowing the terrifying, yet awesome reality, that you are the only person in the world that can do what you were created to do.

Take Action

Write a purpose statement that is no shorter than one sentence and not longer than one paragraph. Your purpose statement should reflect what you believe you are created, called, and purposed to do.

4

Lessons from I Love Lucy

Ages ago, there was a black and white sitcom that literally held the eyes and ears of America. I realize that I am dating myself to some and making myself irrelevant to others, but as a child I became fascinated with watching "I Love Lucy" reruns. On one particular show, Lucy's husband Ricky walks in the house from work and finds Lucy crawling across the floor meticulously looking for something.

"What are you doing?" asks Ricky
Lucy responds, "I am looking for my earrings."
 Ricky inquisitively states, "You lost your earrings in the living room?"
 Lucy then shakes her head no, and asserts, "No, I lost them in the bedroom, but the light out here is much better."

Now, this is funny, but believe it or not it humorously describes so many of our lives. Lucy has decided to make the search easy, while at the same time making the find impossible. In other words, her desire for an easy process has eliminated the possibility of a wanted goal. Now clearly none of us would search for earrings, lost in a bedroom, in a living room .... I don't think. However, there are many of us who have sacrificed effective results, for an easier, more comfortable process. Think about it ... how many times have you decided to go with what was familiar, easier, more known, and more comfortable, but you knew that taking that route would never take where you want to go, place you where you wanted to be, or give you what you wanted to have?

So many of us choose relationships that we know will not ultimately give us happiness, jobs that will not give us purpose, tasks that will not give us fulfillment, all because we want to make it easy on ourselves. Lucy could have made the choice to take a long time to be victorious in a hard search rather than take forever to be defeated in an easy search. How many of us have defeated ourselves because we have chosen the easier path? How many of us will never find what we are looking for because we don't want the frustration of long hours, days, weeks, or months of tireless searching? How many times have we chosen brighter lights only to darken our chances and weaken our future?

Beloved, on today, I want to challenge you to go back to the room where you can find what you are looking for. Go back to the search that may be harder, but ultimately it will be more rewarding. Leave the path that is easier, but offers no victory; rosier, but offers no triumph. If the scripture is true that you reap what you sow, then don't be afraid to till hard ground to get a great harvest.

Take Action

In the next seven days, do something that is uncomfortable for you that will help you get closer to a goal, fulfill a dream, or just move you to a better place in life. (This can include something on your list from the "Stick Your Neck Out" action idea.)

5

The Gospel According to LiL Wayne

A friend of mine let me hear an old interview of Lil Wayne once. He knows how much I like to hear about and hear from people who have achieved greatness in some shape, form, or fashion. Whatever we may say about Lil Wayne's music and personality, most of us have to agree that he is a metaphorical genius and lyrical mastermind. Furthermore, he is in an industry where people constantly flourish and then flounder. Yet, he has found a way to not only survive, but to thrive for over two decades. In the interview, Lil Wayne was giving an account for his prolificacy and said something that caught my ear and has stayed in my thoughts since that moment. Explaining his success, he said (and I am paraphrasing), "Most rappers live in the club and work in the studio. I work in the club and live in the studio." This was his account for the difference and distinction between himself and less successful rappers.

I Loved this reminder for those of us who can look at his multi-platinum, multi-million-dollar success and take for granted that he is just a peculiar talent or just a product of luck. It reminds us that most people who have what we don't have, often have been willing to do what we don't do. It reminds us that great success usually is accompanied and preceded by great work. Lil Wayne says that while most rappers are in the club enjoying the spoils of past work, he is in the studio laying the foundation for future work. In other words, he simply works harder.

Interestingly enough Paul says something similar when talking about the difference between him and his peers. He says in 1 Corinthians 15:10, "But by the grace of God I am what I am, and his grace toward me has not been in vain. On the contrary, I worked harder than any of them ..." Just like Lil Wayne, Paul distinguishes himself from others in his line of duty by pointing to work ethic. Yes, he acknowledges God grace, but he also admits that there is an above and beyond work ethic that separates him from others. This is the gospel ... the gospel of work ethic.

However, what may be good news to some of us may be bad news to a lot of us. When living in a Christian culture that spends so much of its time pleading for a miracle, praising for a breakthrough, and petitioning for deliverance, we can easily believe that our progression in life is waiting on an act of God. On the contrary, many of us need to ask if we are spending too much time in the metaphorical club, and not enough time in the studio. Are we on the couch, when we need to be in the office? Are we hanging with our boys (or girlfriends), when we need to be with our significant other? Are we living for our social life and barely attending to our spiritual life?

Yes, we want greatness—great success, great relationships, great prosperity, and great careers. *But the question is how much are we asking God to work on our deliverance, without delivering on our work?* Thank you, Lil Wayne! Thank you for reminding us that if we don't get where we "live" and where we "work" right, we may be doomed to mediocrity and destined to be a one hit wonder.

Take Action

Make a schedule for your next full week. Each day MAKE TIME to read a book, take a class, practice or do something that will make you better at what you do. (If you find it difficult to come up with something consult a friend, mentor, or role model to help).

6

Vegas and Vision

I Love Las Vegas! The first time I ever visited, I immediately learned what I liked about it the most. It was not the delectable food, the plush hotels, the monstrous buildings, or the overwhelmingly lavish hotels and casinos. It was not even the opportunity to indulge in any conceivable mischief one thousand miles away from home and people who knew me. The single thing that blew me away more than anything was the vision of Las Vegas itself. Vegas sits in the middle of nowhere perched in the midst of a valley. The land was dry, flat, and empty decades ago. Few people thought much of it, and even fewer people decided to live there. Yet years ago, there was a vision to transform a mundane and inconspicuous little town into a booming resort and vacation spot. Now, what once was a bump on the map is now one of the most famous vacation and convention centers in the entire world. That is vision! Whatever you may think about Las Vegas, you must admit that it is the embodiment and result of vision at its best. Vision looks into the future and sees a reality that does not exist in the present. Vision imagines that something can be where nothing exists right now. Vegas is a vision that began in the middle of nowhere. In some ways, vision is a paradox because it is always seeing something that you can not see!

Vegas can teach us so much about having and living with a vision. So many of us shy away from the vision we have for our lives or of our future because it seems to exist in the middle of nowhere. The gap between where we are in the present and what we see in the future is so distant that it scares us away from taking our own vision seriously. The current inaccessibility and present invisibility of what we believe the future can be saps our strength and drains away our devotion to our vision. But every now and then people decide to live in vision, see the unseen, work for the imagined, and commit to making something out of nothing no matter how ridiculous it may seem. The next thing you know you have a place with extravagant hotels, opulent casinos, world championship prize fights, world class concerts, breathtaking shows, and people from all over the world coming to take part. Vision created Vegas. While everyone looked and saw mountains of rocks, miles of sand, and volumes of useless desert plants, there were others who saw what Vegas could be.

In many ways, this is where Vegas meets Jesus (don't be too holy for this!). In the midst of a desert of legalism, rocks of rigid religious regulations, sands of separatism and exclusivity, Jesus had a vision of a spirituality governed by Love and pointed toward inclusivity. Now, just as millions of people tour the Las Vegas strip, billions of people explore their way through the life and teachings of Jesus trying to find meaning and makes sense out of life. Yet, both began with Vision. I want to encourage someone to start taking vision seriously. Refuse to let the current rocks, the present sand, and the existing desert, be a barrier to your imagination. Where you want to go and who you want to be may be in the middle of nowhere, but when you live in vision you can make nowhere become somewhere and nothing become something. VIVA LAS VEGAS!!!

Take Action

Create a vision board that only includes ideas for your future that most people would not see by what they presently know about you. For example, on my board I might put "Song Writer." Most people know me as a pastor and a preacher, but do not know that I have a growing passion to write songs and have already written a few.

7
Looking Up

Some time ago, I was coming from a road trip with one my friends and as we landed back home we found ourselves in the Atlanta airport looking for the baggage claim. In the Atlanta airport, everyone comes from the same train and up the same escalators, then you choose to go to either the north or south sets of baggage claim carousels. There are some six carousels in each terminal, and as we approached the south baggage claim we were about to begin the tedious journey of going from baggage claim to baggage claim looking for our flight number. At worst, this would mean starting in the middle of the carousels, walking to one end, then possibly walking all the way down to the other end in search of the right baggage dispenser. Having traveled slightly more than my buddy, I informed him there was a way to avoid the hassle of treading along carousel to carousel and making numerous wrong stops before finally ending up at our final destination. Above the windows, doors, and carousels there is a screen that has the sole purpose of directing people from their flight to their correct baggage claim. In other words, instead of trying to find our way on our own and using a process of elimination that may be filled with multiple wrong turns, we simply had to look up at the guide to be shown the way.

If you know me by now, then you know that as these words were coming out of my mouth my sermonic antennae went up and my theological telescope began to take focus. What a metaphor for life! How many of us are bumbling and stumbling through life making wrong turn after wrong turn attempting to find our right destination? Many of us continue to make mistake after mistake when we could simply look up and be guided to our desired location.

On one level, finding a model in someone who has gone where we want to go or has done what we want to do is looking up. Unless we are in the elite ranks of Oprah Winfrey, Bill Gates, Warren Buffett, Beyonce, or LeBron James (people who are the best at what they do), there is always someone who serves as a standard whose life can guide us and model for us the path we ought to take. Thus, it behooves us to find models and mentors whose life we can study, and who have the insights and experiences that can save us from trying to make it by ourselves.

On a higher level, we set ourselves up for unnecessary experiments and avoidable mistakes, if we attempt to live life simply searching on the ground level. When we choose to limit our gaze to our mundane world of human desires, paradigms and possibilities, we set ourselves up for mix-ups and mistakes. My friend and I would have bounced around from carousel to carousel had we kept our eyes forward and fixed on the level where we walked. Life mirrors my airport experience in that the best directions call for us to raise our heads and lift our eyes to a place higher than us. In life, the guidance of God always demands that we look up to a loftier place than human experimentation and self-navigation. Such is the case with so many of us who are ending up in dead end places, wrong relationships, and undesirable destinations because we have decided to go place to place looking for our destiny on the ground level. However, looking up to a place beyond us and a Power higher than us may afford us the direction that we so sorely need to rescue us from ourselves.

Take Action

Invite a potential or actual mentor of yours to lunch, coffee, or just a conversation. Interview them about how they sense direction in their life.

8

The Other Door

There I was, in one of the most absolutely necessary and perpetually frustrating places in the world – the security line in the airport. I had just shown my I.D. and boarding pass and was now left to try and guess which scanning line would be the most efficiently run. At this point I began to size up people trying to see who had the most items in their hands and on their shoulders, who looked like they were not going to understand what take your belt off meant, and who was going to have a standoff with their children as the rest of us waited to put our things in a bin. All of a sudden at the end of all the line choices, I spot a doorway that is clearly a further walk, but seemed empty and inviting. So with all the clutter and congestion in the options nearest to me, I decided to go and at least look at this doorway that no one seemed to give a chance. When I got to the entrance, I was amazed to see that the scanning machine was working and readily attended by security guards. To my amazement and excitement, I had the unheard of opportunity to walk unencumbered through security. After a few fist pumps, I began to reflect and my sermonic antenna went up. I realized that I almost missed this opportunity because like most of the people walking through security I did not want to take the walk that was longer, further, and more unknown. All the other security lines were closer and more convenient to approach, but at the same time more crowded. However, because I was willing to walk a little further, I ended up getting where everyone else wanted to go a little faster.

This reminded me of a study done years ago about the psyche of people. At an entryway where there were multiple doors, researchers opened a couple of the doors and let the others stay closed. As crowds began to file in the doorways a crowd emerged at the doors that were already open, and a line was formed. Every now and then someone would take the initiative to try the closed doors and upon realizing that they could just open the door and avoid the line they were able to beat the line. However, upon seeing this, most people STILL chose to stay in the crowd and the congestion at the door that was opened for them instead of going to the doors that were unlocked but required them to open themselves. (I wish somebody knew where I was going and would just meet me there.)

Like my experience in the airport and similar to the research findings about the "other" door, people all over the world continue to stand in crowds that serve as obstacles to their progress and in congestion that impedes their advancement. Yet, often it is the case that if we would walk further on the front end, we can walk freer and faster on the back end. If we would go to the door that takes a little more work, we would find that there are less people there and we could walk into our destiny sooner. Beloved, many of us in life are stagnant and stuck, not because we are devoid of gifts, lack talent, or are without the tools of success. However, we are choosing the road that has less work, that calls for us to walk a shorter distance, or that has already been paved. Yet, I believe the blessings of God and the rewards of life are waiting at the other door. Yes, it's the door you will have to open yourself. Yes, it's the entrance that makes you walk the furthest. And yes, it's the path that will advance you beyond the crowd and propel you above the competition. I pray that in your life you begin to choose the "other" door.

Take Action

Identify three ways doing more or going further could be to your benefit, and choose to do those three things for the next 30 days. (One example could be as simple as not waiting for a close parking spot when you could park further and get more exercise by parking where there is immediate availability.)

9
Walking By Faith

Faith may be the most frequently used, yet hardest to get our practical mind around, word in the Christian vocabulary. The difficulty in grasping faith is not so much defining it, as it is living in it. When we hear the frequently quoted scriptures, "the just shall live by faith (Habakkuk 2:4)" and "without faith it is impossible to please God (Hebrews 11:6)," it becomes clear that faith is extremely important to our spirituality. But recently, when I was asked to talk about faith practically, I must admit that I was initially stumped. If faith is worth its salt you must be able to walk in it. But what does that look like? How does a life of faith "play out?" How does it move beyond simple claims about God's existence, belief in the facts of Jesus' life, or even intellectual assent to the wondrous works of the Creator?

The other Sunday I received the beginning of an answer in one of the simply worded melodic classics of the church. Growing up as a boy few Sundays went by without some rendition of the profoundly timeless hymn, "I Will Trust in the Lord." This song, whose title is the content of the first verse, begins by making a statement of faith that is followed with a verse by verse fleshing out of what a life of faith looks like. Consider some of the verses:

"I am going to treat everybody right."
"I am going to stay on the battlefield."
"I am going to watch, fight, and pray."

The majesty of this song cannot be understood without some understanding of its setting. This song comes out of the hearts of a people suffering from the violence of American slavery and the zenith of racial oppression. In a world with political inequality, rape, and human brutalization people defiantly sang the second verse that says, "I am going to treat everybody right." Really?!!? Why would such a "wronged" people declare they would live with a universal commitment to "right" treatment? This only makes sense if there is a loftier way of living, a Higher way of thinking, and a Transcendent reality to which their actions appealed. Likewise, in the following verses, "I am going to stay on the battlefield," and "I am going to watch, fight and pray," speak to a choice of commitments that would seem to have been futile without political, military, or economic power. When you live in a world where you are constantly being treated wrong and you are powerless by most identifiable measures, choosing to swim against the tide, go against the grain, and commit yourself to practices that have no visible results is to walk by faith. Put another way, Black people's choice to Love their wider community, their country, and themselves is a prime example of faith.

Sitting in church the other day I listened to the praise team sing this song, and as they went through the verses a theological lightbulb began to pop up in my mind. *Walking by faith is living as if there is something higher than our hands can grasp, better than our eyes can see, and deeper than our senses can feel.* Living in faith is to refuse to be tyrannized by the visible, swept away by conventional wisdom, or consumed by "common" sense. It is making the choice to listen for a call that gives fulfillment instead of searching for a career that guarantees finances. It is choosing Love over power, acceptance over xenophobia, giving over greed, and community over individualism. Walking by faith is to connect one's actions to commitments that do not always have immediate gratification or instant manifestations. As the great Negro Spiritual understood, "trusting in the Lord" is defined by one's endeavors and not one's claims.

Live Greater

Take Action

Make a faith list. Write a list of things you could or should commit to that you believe are better for you and the world even if they do not yield immediate, visible, or tangible results.

10
The Power of Next

Some time ago, I was given a book entitled "Golf Is Not a Game of Perfect." Since my attempts at golf have already made me painfully aware of this fact, and because I believe golf is a lot like life, I began reading as soon as I could. Dr. Bob Rotella, a respected and renowned Sports psychologist, writes with Bob Cullen to give insights and ideas to help readers with the mental aspect of their golf game. As I suspected, there is so much in the book that is relevant to and reflective of life.

In the first chapter, a chapter devoted to discussing dreams, a very powerful point is made by the example of two golfers. One such golfer is none other than the golf legend (from the great state of Texas by the way) Byron Nelson. Looking back on his career, Nelson realized what made him great when he was great. He said when he was a young player he dreamed of owning a ranch, and every time he played he was playing to buy property, fence it, build a house on it, furnish the house, build barns and corrals, fill them with animals, hire someone to care for it while he was touring, then stash money aside to take care of it forever. Interestingly, once his dream was realized and the ranch was all paid for, Nelson said, "I pretty much stopped playing. I was all but done as a competitive player."

The other golfer, Pat Bradley, was inspired by a detailed dream to "win more ... win majors ... be Player of the Year at least once .... And be in the LPGA Hall of Fame." This requires winning at least thirty tournaments and one of them a major, making it one of the hardest Hall of Fame's to enter. She told these dreams to Dr. Rotella in the early 80's, and in 1991 she was inducted into the Hall of Fame. At the very induction ceremony she approached Dr. Rotella, who was there to support her, and said, "Where do we go from here? Bob, we've got to find a new dream. What's next?"

Both of these stories in some form speak to the necessity of a "next" in our lives. Byron Nelson realized that his competitive edge left and his reign on top of the golf world ended because he did not have a "next" in his mind. On the other hand, Pat Bradley illustrates that it is never too early to begin thinking about what is next. Whether we are dealing with failure on the stage of success, or stuck in the middle, the progress of our lives and the growth of our spirituality demand that we have a sense of next. Without it, our drive can be drained, our cause can be crippled, and our strength can be sapped. The idea of "next" gives us the fuel to keep fighting and the motivation to keep moving.

In Philippians 3:13-14, after Paul has reflected on his socio-religious accomplishments, he says, "forgetting what lies behind and straining forward to what lies ahead, I press on toward the goal..." This is what the power of "next" does for us. In the face of failures that may have suffocated our spirit, or success that may have taken away our drive, "next" gives us the amnesia we need to get excited and focus on what God has for us in our future. So no matter how many times you have fallen or how many goals you have already reached, you should always ask yourself, "What's next?"

Take Action

Identify or create a goal, or a list of goals, that you want to accomplish sometime after the things you have going on in your life presently. It may be goals you have after retirement, after your degree is completed, or after a current project you are working on is finished.

11
Spirituality

In the final chapter of his book, Days of Grace, Arthur Ashe wrote to his daughter: "Camera, have faith in God. Do not be tempted whether by pleasures and material possessions, or by the claims of science and smart thinkers, into believing that religion is obsolete, that the worship of God is somehow beneath you. Spiritual nourishment is as important as physical nourishment and intellectual nourishment." This profound parting advice still provides us with a relevant message. In a Christian culture where so many are religious (followers of the regular routine of church, events, and celebrations), pious (followers of strict codes of behavior and diet), and/or holy (content to set themselves apart from the "sinners" and secularity of the world), we need a renewed focus on spirituality.

I often define spirituality as taking care of the homes that take care of us. Our spirit is the home of our relationship with God, and our mind and bodies are the homes of our spirit. Spirituality is taking care of these homes. All of us know that homes need maintenance, cleaning, repair, and upgrading. Wherever we live, we have to vacuum the carpet, sweep the floors, dust the furniture, change the air filters, mow the lawn, wash the dishes, etc .... You get the point! However, such is the case in our spiritual lives. Our mind, body, and spirit need care, cleaning, and nurturing so that we can have a healthy environment for our connection and communion with God.

Spirituality is more important than being religious, pious, or holy. Because no matter how much church we attend, how many moral codes we observe, or how many people or places we think are beneath us, when tough times and tough decisions come our way we need an invisible, intangible, foundation that will guide, comfort, and keep us. When we suffer the loss of a loved one, the loss of our job, or contraction of a critical illness only that which is deep inside of us can keep us calm, give us peace, or preserve our sanity. When we must make the tough decision between the pain of a bad relationship or the loneliness of no relationship we need something deep inside of us to push us to the right decision no matter how painful it may be. Spirituality is found in the actions we take and the practices we commit to nurturing our mind, body, and our spirit. It is found in our commitment to eat well and exercise consistently. It is found when we take time to read, study, pray, fast, meditate, worship, and live in intentional forms of community. Spirituality is not simply a set of faith claims and intellectual ideas. Ideas may form the foundation of our spirituality, but they do not form the substance of it. Ideas cannot nourish, only action and practice can do that.

Even more, spirituality is the key to a profound form of greatness that lives longer than us, reaches further than us, and grows bigger than us. This greatness can only be achieved when we make our lives about more than just ourselves. Connecting to something other than yourself (God, others, and great causes) is in part related to living for something greater than yourself. So, I challenge you today to not allow your spirituality to go unattended, untouched, or undone. Your greatness depends on it.

Take Action

Choose a practice (prayer, fasting, exercise, meditation, etc.) to do and a cause to give your commitment. Carve out a part of your day and begin implementing that practice daily, no matter what. Then look at your calendar and think about your commitments.

Live Greater

Find something you can do three times in the next thirty days that will be you giving your time and energy to something bigger than you.

12

You Can't Get Extraordinary Without Ordinary

"Let go and let God" is one of the most deceptive clichés in Christians' vocabulary. We hear it all the time, we say it all the time, but living it can be to our danger and our detriment. There is a story in the Bible where Moses attempted to let go and let God and you may be amazed at what happens: God won't have it!

We have all heard the story of the parting of the Red Sea. However, few of us talk about the conflict between Moses and God right before the miracle. In the 14th chapter of Exodus the story of Moses' liberation of the Israelites picks up right after they have escaped from Egypt. As Pharaoh's army gets near, the Israelites are stuck with the Red Sea in front of them and the Egyptian army behind them. At this point, they turn on Moses and begin questioning his leadership and his entire attempt at liberating them in the first place. Then Moses, in an attempt to encourage and quiet the people says, "Do not be afraid, stand firm and see the deliverance that the Lord will accomplish for you today ... The Lord will fight for you, and you have only to keep still (Exodus 14:13-14 NRSV)." It looks like Moses is definitely trying to let go and let God.

The problem is that God interrupts Moses and says this, "Why do you cry out to me? Tell the Israelites to go forward. But you lift up your staff, and stretch out your hand over the sea and divide it. That the Israelites may go into the sea on dry ground (Exodus 14:15-16 NRSV)." WE HAVE A PROBLEM!!! Moses has told the Israelites to stand still and be still and God will act, but

God says Moses needs to act and the Israelites need to keep moving. God will not allow them to let go and let God.

So many of us are between rocks and hard places in our lives and it would be so easy to be still and stand still and wait on God to fight for us. We are waiting on a miraculous move and an extraordinary breakthrough, but God may be looking at us and telling us to "lift up our staff, and stretch out our hand." Moses was trying to pass the buck, when with his own hand and what was in his hand, he had what he needed to initiate a miracle. The extraordinary event of the splitting of the Red Sea happened through the lifting of an ordinary staff and the stretching of an ordinary hand. Too often we are waiting on God to move, while we keep still the ordinary gifts and graces God has given us. The truth is you cannot get extraordinary without ordinary. God has given you an ordinary mind, an ordinary talent, ordinary hands that if you would just use them, they could yield extraordinary results. So, don't ask for God's EXTRA, if you have not used your ordinary.

Take Action

Most of us have situations we have identified as beyond our control. Think of something you have determined to be out of your hands, or too big for you to handle. Then, write a list of all the things you can do to affect the circumstance in any shape, form, or fashion. Finally, set a schedule or action plan to do all the things you have identified as within your power.

13

It's Not Whether You Win or Lose ...

I have a new and profound respect for Oprah Winfrey. There are many things that make her worthy of adulation and that claim my admiration. She is probably the most successful talk show host of all times. She has endured a childhood of abuse and early adult low self-esteem to become one of the most powerful and multi-dimensional people in the media industry. She has also established a legacy through her commitment to utilizing black people and telling black people's stories through the arts. Finally, she has been a major philanthropic presence throughout the world. Yet, there is something else far more mundane that grabbed my attention and admiration a while back.

A few years ago, I was watching Good Morning America and it reported that Oprah has gone public with her battle with weight loss. For more than twenty years Oprah has had a public back and forth struggle with losing and gaining weight. She has appeared on TV with fat in a wagon demonstrating how much weight she has lost, only to gain in all back in a matter of a few years. This cycle has happened more than once and at the time of GMA's story Oprah weighed in excess of two hundred pounds. While tabloids may find this entertaining, I am so very proud, impressed, and inspired by Oprah's public acknowledgement of this personal battle. I am proud because it demonstrates a profound spiritual point.

All of us have some vice that we cannot seem to kick. Oprah's weight is some of our low self-esteem, another's sexual promiscuity, someone else's laziness and procrastination, or lying, cheating, low ambition, lack of drive, selfishness, addiction, etc..... You get the point! However, unlike Oprah in the case of her weight, some of us have lost the desire to fight against the vices that hold us back or keep us down in one way or another. Too often we give in to our weakness and quit under the guise of "accepting ourselves." I mean, imagine that after twenty years Oprah still is going back and forth with her weight. Over twenty years of struggle! Yet she still musters enough courage to go to battle with that which ails her and temporarily defeats her. I love it! I love it because this is an example of spiritual strength and human frailty at its best and most real.

The truth of the matter is there are things in life that seem to get the best of us over and over again. Somewhere along the way we lose the desire, the discipline, and/or the determination to look that which plagues us in the face and continue to fight. *Oprah has yet to decisively beat her weight problem, but as long as she continues to fight, her weight problem has not decisively beat her.* This is the case with all of us as long as we continue to fight our vices. I want to encourage someone today to keep fighting. As long as you keep fighting, whatever it is that has seemed to get the best of you cannot claim victory in your life. Sometimes the victory is in the fight. No, it does not always mean we conquer our spiritual and personal enemies, but it does mean we resist their ability to conquer us. This is the spiritual point that has garnered my affection and admiration for Oprah. It's not always whether you win or lose; it is your decision to stay in the game. Keep fighting!!!

Take Action

Resume a fight you have given up. Whether it's weight loss, eating more healthy, budgeting better, or reading more, find something you have let go and try again.

14

Ready or Not

Most people would agree that they are not living up to their spiritual or life potential in some aspect or area of their lives. And when asked, "why not", one of the most common responses is because "I am not ready." Whether it is making a deeper commitment to our spirituality, breaking a bad habit, stopping the cycle of addiction, getting another degree, starting a business, committing to a relationship, or moving from a career to a call, it is hard to ever feel ready to move to the next level in life. "I am not ready to make the sacrifices." "I am not ready to make changes in my lifestyle." "I am not ready to give up this or that." The truth of the matter is we are usually not "ready" to meet the demands of our destiny and live up to the terms of our greatness.

Our history is filled with people who were thrust into places and positions before they felt they were ready. Martin Luther King Jr. went to Montgomery, Alabama to pastor a modest sized Dexter Avenue Baptist Church, when all of a sudden he was thrust into the leadership of the National Civil Rights Movement. King often communicated that at times he felt overwhelmed by the task and not particularly ready for that amount of responsibility. Gardner Taylor, who Ebony deemed at one point the greatest black preacher in America, always testified that as a Pastor of a church in Louisiana he did not feel ready to make the monumental move to assume the Pastorate at the historic Concord Baptist Church in New York, New York.

Taylor says something very insightful about readiness. He profoundly exhorts that when God calls us to the next level of our destiny we are almost never ready. Yet he suggests that if we just trust God and move into our call, God makes us ready in the process. I want to encourage someone today to make a move for the better that up until this point you have convinced yourself that you are not ready to make, but in the depths of your heart you know it is a move that you need to make. It may be a general move like loving harder, giving more, praying more, reading more, studying more intensely, living more healthy, or increasing your commitment to your spiritual life. It may also be something specific like joining a church, changing careers, letting a relationship go, forming a new relationship, or becoming an entrepreneur. Even if you feel you are not quite developed for your destiny, I want you to trust in a God who can develop you on the way to your destiny. So, ready or not, make your move.

Take Action

Read the last paragraph again and make a decision to start a specific behavior or make a specific new commitment.

15

Stuck in the Middle

---

22) They came to Bethsaida. Some people brought a blind man to him and begged him to touch him. 23) He took the blind man by the hand and led him out of the village; and when he had put saliva on his eyes and laid his hands on him, he asked him, "Can you see anything?" 24) And the man looked up and said, "I can see people, but they look like trees, walking." 25) Then Jesus laid his hands on his eyes again; and he looked intently and his sight was restored, and he saw everything clearly. (Mark 8: 22-25 NRSV)

This is one of the most interesting healing stories in the Bible as I see it. On one hand, it is interesting because Jesus touches a blind man who is given sight, but can still not see clearly. It is the only miracle story where there is a healing that takes two touches. For theologians, Biblical scholars, or those of us who think critically, this raises all kinds of interesting theological questions. Why didn't the first touch heal the blind man completely? Does this tell us something about the limits of Jesus? How can an all-powerful Jesus touch someone and they not be able to see well? These kinds of questions have been and will be debated for centuries.

However, not only does the intellectual side of me find this story interesting, the experiential side of me that lives in a real world everyday Loves this story. Imagine all that must have been going on with this man in the moment where he has been touched by Jesus, but he is not completely healed. Sight has been improved, but it has not been fully restored. Sight has progressed, but it has not been perfected. Maybe this man was joyful for the ability to see anything. Maybe he was frustrated that after all this time of waiting and wanting to see, he can now see, but he cannot see clearly.

Here is where this story hits me the hardest. I believe much of our lives exist somewhere between these two touches. Many of us know what it is to have real encounters with God, and just as many of us know what it is for our lives to still not be perfected. Like this blind man, we have had authentic encounters with God, yet life is still not exactly where we would like it to be. So many issues in our lives, habits of our lives, and situations throughout our lives are somewhere between these two touches. Somewhere between "not what it used to be" and "not what we want it to be." This blind man has experienced the healing power of Jesus, and yet this blind man is not completely healed. Today, we may be able to confess that God has touched us, healed us, spoken to us, and/or kept us. Nevertheless we still struggle, things are still not clear, all is still not well and life is still not complete. In some area and aspect of our lives, we are stuck in the middle between progress and perfection.

This blind man serves as a lesson to all of us who may be "stuck in the middle" of two touches today. Jesus only asks him, "Can you see anything?" The man could have said "yes" and been satisfied with his current state. Yet, he clearly was not satisfied. He was not content to simply be better when there was more to be fulfilled. So he takes the initiative to tell Jesus something that Jesus does not even ask. "And the man looked up and said, "I can see people, but they look like trees, walking." This initiative moves Jesus to touch him again. His initiative allows him to leave with fully recovered sight.

Beloved, I don't know where you are or what you are going through but I guarantee you don't have to look far to find some aspect of your life that is stuck in the middle of two touches. I hope you are encouraged today not to be satisfied. If the vision is not clear, the dream is not fulfilled, the expectation is not met, or you are not completely healed, then please don't be satisfied. Take the initiative to keep fighting, keep working, keep striving, keep pressing, and keep praying and telling God exactly where you are and what you need. Make the move, take the step, and live with initiative. The second touch may be on the way.

Take Action

Write a prayer to God about the places you have seen God work, but are not completely healed. Articulate what is incomplete about the current picture, and remind God (and really yourself) that you want more.

16
Accelerate

I drive a lot … a whole lot! I live west of Atlanta, pastor a church in Fayetteville, GA that is south of Atlanta, and have a child who goes to school north of Atlanta. For four years my wife lived in Winston-Salem, NC and twice a month I drove there. One year I bought a new car in August and by the following January, I had almost put 30,000 miles on my car. For this reason, I bought a Ford Fusion Hybrid. Had I not, on any given day you may have found me on the highway with a sign that read, "Will Preach for Gas Money." I thoroughly enjoyed the Hybrid as it saved me some $200-$300 in gas each month. There is only one part of the Hybrid I do not like … it has little to NO get up and go.

One of the great things about my car is that it can tell you during each tank of gas how many miles per gallon you are averaging. Because of this, I have realized how hills, traffic, and highways affect gas mileage. However, the one thing that drives my gas mileage per gallon down more than anything else is acceleration. Whenever I accelerate, my car uses more energy, effort and gas than at any other time. My car spends less gas driving consistently at 80 mph (not that I drive that fast, wink) than it does getting to 80mph. Do not drive by this point because there is a principle here. It takes more effort and energy to gain speed than it does to keep the speed we gain.

This sounds simple enough when it comes to cars, but we miss this very fundamental point all the time in our lives. So much of our growth, success, and happiness is based on our ability to change speed. The power to break the habit, change our lifestyle, or initiate a new practice is dependent on changes of speed. However, many of us are trying to change our lives without changing our speed. We want greater results without greater effort, to have more without doing more, or radical change with minimal energy. Unfortunately, we bring God into this by exercising a "let go and let God" strategy, where we hope, pray, and plead for God to make us go faster without burning any of our own gas.

So, I've got tough news for you. It may be you are not going where you want to go as fast as you want to get there because you are more interested in saving gas than burning gas. It is true that getting to a higher speed is the most exhausting thing in the world. Accelerating in life will take more out of you, drain more from you and ask more of you than anything in the world. You will be more tired! You will lose more sleep! You will have less energy! However, just like my Hybrid, our ability to maintain at a high speed takes less energy than getting there. Once we get the degree, improve the marriage, get the business up and running, make the spiritual habit, life does offer us moments to go in cruise control. Now of course living life at 80mph, takes more than living life at 20mph. But it is the getting to 80 that takes the most energy. The next move in your life will only be as great as the extra energy you are willing to exert. So get some sleep, eat a good breakfast, get in the car, and gas up!

Take Action

Choose an area of your life where you need to gain speed and make a 30, 60, or 90-day commitment to giving more energy toward that area.

17
Finding Balance

Phoenix, Arizona is one of the most interesting cities in the U.S. On more than one occasion, I have had the pleasure of visiting this retirement and vacationing hot bed while participating in a pastor's retreat. The first time I was leaving I found myself taking in its unique beauty one last time as my flight was taking off. As I looked down, it dawned on me that I could not remember visiting many major cities in the continental United States with mountains sprinkled in the midst of the city. I have written about my Love for the beauty of Vegas which is situated in a valley and almost surrounded by mountains. Yet, in Phoenix there are mountains dabbled right there in the middle of the city.

As I watched the contrast between the mountains and valleys of Phoenix, it dawned on me that wherever there were mountains, residential life was few and far between. Residential life had to pause for the mountains. There was something about the terrain, the verticality, and the rockiness of the mountains that was hostile to roads, houses, and businesses. You could hike up some parts of the mountains. You could even climb up the mountains, but you could not take residence there. There was something beautiful about the balance between the mountains and the valleys of Phoenix. There was also something enlightening about this combination.

It began to dawn on me, right there at my window seat, that I was looking at a life lesson right before my eyes. The beauty of Phoenix was in the fact that it had managed to combine, balance if you will, places where you could climb with places where you could live. Mountains serve as a metaphor to parts of us that want to achieve, while valleys serve as places where we live as social selves. We achieve through our pursuit of education, entrepreneurship, and careers. Yet, our social lives are far more about being and experiencing than they are about "achieving." Unfortunately, for some obsessive climbers, their social lives become solely about their climb. Finding balance is so often difficult to find in the lives of people. There are those of us in life whose entire lives are dedicated to climbing mountains. Our lives become one big pursuit, quest for achievement, and/or search for the next pinnacle. To the contrary, others of us would simply live in a world of social valleys where we can live a flat existence without the desire to achieve any real feat or climb to any great height. Our lives either become mountain-less valleys, or a constant range of mountains, either characterized by the contentment of routine, rest, and repetition, or marked by endless pursuits of new climbs.

Yet Phoenix reminds us of the beauty of finding a way to live amongst mountains and valleys. It reminds us that each have their beauty and their purpose. Mountains are made to climb, but we cannot build there; they give us a place to accomplish, but we cannot live there. So many of us attempt to make a life of constant climbing and make our lives exclusively about our pursuits. Our lives become solely about achievement with no place to rest, live, and just be. Many of us have climbed mountain after mountain, but we have never made a home. Others of us have never felt the thrill of mountaineering. We have never challenged ourselves to enjoy the striving, struggle, and strain of reaching a peak.

In the end, I believe Phoenix has it right. Life is truly beautiful when we allow mountains and valleys to co-exist in the midst of the traffic of our lives. Our lives are so much more when we insist on making achievement a part of our lives, but we refuse to allow our mountains to be all of our lives.

Take Action

Make a schedule for your next week or your next month and make sure you are intentional in your attempt to both achieve and find time with family and friends to simply exist.

18

Take Responsibility

2012 ended with one of the most tragic mass shootings of my life time. On December 14, 20 students and 6 adults were murdered at Sandy Hook Elementary School. Understandably, we began to ask ourselves, who or what was to blame for this tragedy. Was it gun control or the lack thereof in our country? Was it our insensitivity or lack of proficiency in dealing with the mentally impaired? Was it a media that unintentionally glamorizes the perpetrators of these mass killings and thus sets a new bar for potential killers? Was it a violent murderous culture where violent deaths are highlighted in movies, video games, and television series? On one hand, there was a lot of potential blame to pass around, but on the other hand, no one wants to take the blame.

Yet, as we look into and attempt to build a better future, we soon find that blame about the past is less important than responsibility for the future. The lessons from tragedy always beseech us to be courageous enough to create a better world. We don't have to accept blame for a tragedy happening in order to take responsibility for preventing it from happening again.

We are now left with the questions about what kind of world we will continue to live in and construct. What will we do about the proliferation of guns and gun violence? How will we care, Love, and nurture the mentally impaired? When will our media become more responsible, or be made to be more responsible? These are the questions for those of us who will be courageous enough to respond to issues that we did not create, work on problems that we did not cause, and fight for causes that do not directly affect us. The past failures of children may not be our fault, but their future success can be our responsibility.

This communal principle also speaks to us individually as we set goals and map out our plans for our future. Many of us might be honest enough to admit that we often find ourselves with imperfect lives, unwanted realities, and unfair situations that we did not cause. Some part, if not most parts, of our lives are not what or where we would have them. Unfortunately, when we find ourselves dealing with undesirable circumstances, we can spend too much time assessing who is to blame for the problems, issues, and troubles of our life. Such is the case with a CEO who is brought in to turn a company around. She or he is put in a place where they are usually not responsible for the flaws and failures of the company. Nevertheless, the future success of the company becomes their responsibility even if the past failures is not their fault. I want to challenge you to use your life taking responsibility for what you want to do and where you want to go no matter who or what is responsible for where you are. I pray that we would believe that bettering our selves, community, nation, and world is our responsibility, even if all that we inherit is not our fault. Yesterday may not have been in your control, but today and tomorrow are your responsibility. Take it! Make it! Own it!

Take Action

Make a commitment to use your energy, time, and/or talents improving something or someone that is not naturally connected to you. Some examples would be:

- mentoring a child that is not your own
- a younger person working on an elderly issue or an elderly person working on an issue that impacts children
- attempting to help make a solution to a problem you did not cause at work, church, or in your community

19

Getting Over What's Beneath You

Often, the very things that we think are beneath us are the missing pieces to the next level of progress and the next rung of success in our lives. This was confirmed for me while reading one of Patrick Lencioni's books, The Advantage. In this book, Lencioni contends that the number one competitive advantage for any company, organization, school, or institution is organizational health. The problem, he argues, is that most leaders ignore organizational health "even though it is simple, free, and available to anyone who wants it." For years, he wondered why this was the case, and on July 28, 2010, he heard one of the best answers. Lencioni was at a client's leadership conference, sitting next to the CEO and listening to presentation after presentation about the unique and unorthodox activities that made this company one of the most healthy and successful organizations over the last fifty years. Lencioni asked this executive, "Why in the world don't your competitors do any of this?" A few seconds later, the executive whispered to him, "You know, I honestly believe they think it's beneath them." Lencioni then concludes, "In spite of its undeniable power, so many leaders struggle to embrace organizational health ... because they quietly believe they are too sophisticated, too busy, or too analytical to bother with it." So many leaders reduce the running of their companies to strategy, marketing, finance, and technology, while not paying attention to relationship, morale, politics, and employee turnover because they don't want to get into the touchy-feely aspects of leadership. The intangible, non-quantifiable, relational aspects of their companies are beneath them. However, these same issues can and often do become the downfall of the company.

As I read this, I began to think of how many times, how many ways, and in how many situations we end up with less than optimal lives because we have deemed something beneath us. The bonding time fathers lose with their infants because changing diapers, feeding, or waking up in the middle of the night is a "woman's" job. Consider the couples that struggle in their relationships because addressing emotions, being vulnerable, or just getting counseling is not for them. Think about the churches that miss opportunities for real ministry because sophisticated Christians don't want to get their hands dirty with people who are too sick, too poor, or too uneducated for their tastes; or the person with pain, hurt, anger, or addiction who is too in control to get help. If we really dig deep and search ourselves, there is something we have determined to be beneath us that would help us deeply, improve us greatly, and benefit us significantly.

The Bible warns us about these same issues in Proverbs 16:18 when it says, "Pride goes before destruction, and a haughty spirit before the fall." Beloved, each of us has something we have decided is beneath us that we need to get over. In the end our rise may be determined by how low we can stoop to attend to the "little" things that will make all the difference.

Take Action

Read this reflection again with someone who knows you well and Loves you deeply. Then have a conversation with each other about the things you have deemed beneath you that could help you become better.

20
GO!

An evangelical story is told about the devil talking with his demons and they are strategizing about how they can keep people from living in and with a relationship with God. The first demon suggests that they try to convince people that God is not real. The devil decides that though this may work for some, however, the majesty and mystery of life will always drive many people to believe there is more. He concludes this would not be the best strategy and this approach will not suffice. Another demon says let me go and tell them that heaven is not real. The devil thinks it through, weighs the pros and cons, but ultimately decides this would not be the optimal strategy to keep people from their spiritual best. Finally, a demon gets up and says, "I know what to do. I will not tell them God is not real, and I will not tell them that heaven is not real. What I will do is assure them that they do in fact need a relationship with God, but I will just tell them to wait. I will convince them that tomorrow would be a better time than today. I will assure them that they should wait until they do one more thing, break one more habit, or have one more pleasurable experience. Then, when the time comes for them to get closer to God I'll make up another reason they should wait." Of course, the devil decides this is the best strategy.

Whatever you make think about the story, isn't it easy to relate to the principle that one of the things that keeps us from being our best selves is intentional or unintentional procrastination. It is not that we do not know, believe, or accept what we should do. It is just we always find some reasonable explanation to wait. In fact, if we really took inventory, we would find that procrastination and hesitation are two habits that have been the most destructive to our lives. Yes, procrastination, not lack of talent or a dearth of potential, is many of our biggest enemy. It's not that we can't or believe we shouldn't, it is simply that we haven't …. YET (at least this is what we tell ourselves).

Over and over again we find that some of the most successful people in life are those who resisted that specious voice that says, "stop," "hold on," "not right now," and/or "wait." Often, there is no real talent gap between us and those who thrive. There is simply in them the instinct to GO and not WAIT. Nevertheless, we continue to find reasons to hesitate on fulfilling our potential, realizing our dreams, reaching for our destinies, and achieving our goals. Right now there are so many of us that know a task needs to be done, a relationship needs ending, an apology needs to be given, a habit needs to be stopped, but somehow we can convince ourselves that this is not the time, we don't have the time, there will be another time, or we will wait until the next time.

Yet today I hope that you be filled with the spirit of GO. I write this not just as a giver of this word, but as someone who needs this word in my life. I remember when I initially wrote this it was at the end of the week, and I was tempted by the idea that it would be better to wait until Monday to send it. For whatever reason, I thought it would be better to send this kind of message on a Monday. In fact, I cannot count the things that we put off, thinking somehow that Monday is this magical day that will allow us to actually get our lives together. I want to encourage you to do something this day, in this moment, and at this time that will move you forward, take you upward, and push you onward. When it comes to doing the next right thing in your life, the time is now, the starting point is here, and the thing to do is GO!

Take Action

Stop right now and attend to something or some task where you have been procrastinating. Even if you just take 5 minutes to start, do it now. Maybe it's a call you have been hesitating to make or a conversation you have been reticent to have. Whatever it is .... Do something now! If you have thought about starting a business or non-profit, go read one article about it right now. Go!!!

21
Keep Going!

In the previous reflection, I attempted to convince you of the importance and value of simply beginning a task, starting a work, and initiating an action. I encouraged you to resist the temptation to "wait" that so often keeps us from moving closer to our destiny. However, it would be naïve for us to think that all we have to do is start in order to reach the finish line. I was reminded of this myself the other day while reading a tweet that said, most overnight successes took twenty years to get here. In other words, when we see a person achieving fame or a company saturating the market, there are usually years of struggle, strife, and strain that precede their accomplishment.

Consider the story of Christianity. When Christianity began it was simply a grassroots, marginalized religion filled with poor, illiterate, and persecuted people. It was a knock off of Judaism initiated by some plebian carpenter who was born and raised in the ghetto and who died on death row. For years Christians were seen as a weird group of poor people with strange practices and very little status in the world. For almost three centuries Emperors took turns attempting to wipe the religion and its adherents out. Then, in a twist of fate that changed the landscape of religious history in the world, Constantine declared himself a Christian and made Christianity the religion of the largest empire of that era. All of a sudden, it began to be fashionable, in some places, to be a Christian. The truth is however, "all of a sudden" really was about three hundred years. Today, Christianity is one of the largest religions on the face of the earth, and it's easy to think that Jesus came and in one swipe changed everything. However, have you thought about that first three hundred years? We live in a country that is not even 250 years old, and think of all the things that have happened during that time. Native Americans have been displaced, wars have been fought, Africans have been captured, enslaved, and dislocated from their home land, enslaved Africans have been emancipated. Then, after emancipation, the same country that chained black people over a century ago was run by an African American for eight years. In both the case of Christianity and America, there were decades of struggle, strife, and strain before change came.

Such is the case in our lives. Though it sounds good for breakthrough to come in a blink of an eye, it usually never does. The truth is, most great companies, most great institutions, and most great people went through times when they thought they would not make it. Moreover, these times were not just fleeting moments or bad weekends. Often they were weeks, months, and even years. This is why we so often combine the wisdom writer in Ecclesiastes with the New Testament imperative to say "the race is not given to the swift, nor the battle to the strong … but to the one who endures to the end." Beloved, your success will not just be about what you can do; it will be about what you can go through. Your victory will not just be about the riches you receive; it will be about the poverty you can endure. Once you decide to start, then you must dedicate yourself to suffering through whatever challenges lay on your path to destiny. Once you decide to go, your triumph will be determined by your ability to keep going. So, even as you are in the midst of an undesirable circumstance, an unwanted situation, and/or an unwelcome reality, stay with it, stay on it, and stay at it!!! Don't just go …. KEEP GOING!

Take Action

Either choose one area of your life, or look at your life generally, and make one, five, and ten year goals.

22
Focus

Does anybody go to public pools anymore? When I was growing up in Austin, Texas this was one of our favorite summer activities. However, when we did not have the means (read transportation or money) to go to the pool, we had a supplemental activity that we called "getting wet." Getting wet was when friends around the neighborhood would put on their bathing suits, meet in someone's yard, and pull out the water hose. We would literally take turns holding the water hose and spraying each other with it, and somehow we thought this was a good time—a great time in fact. We were always challenged to see who could get the water to go the furthest and shoot out the hardest. Of course, this was done by covering the mouth of the hose with your thumb and allowing the built up pressure to shoot the water out with force.

Though we did not know it then, we were demonstrating a scientific principle and illustrating a life principle. Scientifically, we were taking advantage of the relationship between pressure and power. Force, speed, and power can be generated by pressure. We were creating more force, speed, and power by narrowing the exit point of the water. Essentially, we were giving the water hose more focus. We could make the water go further, faster, and move with more force if we used our thumb to make the exit point more focused.

This principle is all the more true in our lives. God gives us expertise, energies, and experiences that build in us and are waiting to be released into the world. Many of us leak out these resources with no aim, ambition, or intention. They come out in a conversation here and there. We may use them for a project at our church, an event for a social organization of which we are a member, or even a task at our job. However, we have yet to find a singular passion or purpose for which we can channel the resources gifted to us by God and afforded by life. Just like the water in a hose sprays out further, faster, and with more force when it is channeled more narrowly, our lives are more powerful, prolific, and profound when we focus our energies.

The sad reality for many of us is that our lives are so spread out, our efforts are so disconnected, and our time is so disjointed that we never generate the force and impact our lives are meant to have. Our existence has no real focus! No wonder we make no major mark, leave no lasting legacy, and craft no meaningful change. The exit point for our energies is too wide. At an informal dinner the father of Bill Gates asked his son and Warren Buffet, two of the richest and most successful men in the world, what was the single most important factor in their success? Both gave the same answer—their focus. The difference between average and amazing, mediocre and marvelous, ordinary and outstanding is usually not talent and potential. It is focus. So, find a dream, adopt a cause, and/or pursue a purpose that is worth receiving the bulk of your attention and channeling the lion's share of your effort. God has not created us to do everything, but God has crafted us to do something. Find it! Follow it! Focus on it.

Take Action

Identify one passion/dream in your life that should be getting some of your time every day. Now make time every day to FOCUS on this for the next 90 days. Evaluate your progress and take note of how you feel at the end.

23

When It's Cold Outside

The other day, I overheard someone on their cell phone explaining to the person on the other end of the line how beautiful a day it was and how the temperature was going to be in the fifties. This person was right and wrong. On one hand, the day was absolutely stunning. The sun was blazing and beaming its illustrious light across the landscape of the earth, and the sky was a breathtaking blue only interrupted by the occasional plush, puffy, and pure white cloud. On the other hand, the temperature never rose above 33 degrees. It took me back to my childhood when I would look outside on a bright, winter day and see nothing but sunshine, blue skies, and white clouds. Inevitably, I would get excited and anticipate a warm day. However, I would always be surprised when I went outside and experienced chilling temperatures and frigid winds. I was consumed and confused by the paradox of an outside that looked bright, warm, and sunny, but felt cold, chilling, and frigid. Eventually, nature taught me the eternal truth—how things look don't always line up with how they feel.

Isn't it amazing that some of us are still learning this truth in other areas of our lives? Many of us chose a path, a partner, or a profession because they looked profitable, rewarding, upwardly mobile, and impressive. We chose a career path because we knew the house we wanted to live in, the car we wanted to drive, and the figures we wanted to see on our check. But, after working for years, attaining numerous degrees, or politicking our way through promotion after promotion, we find ourselves struggling to be happy about going to work. Moreover, we find ourselves asking, "What's the point?" Our resume still looks bright and sunny, but our spirit is cold. Maybe we chose a partner because on paper this person could not have been a better fit. They have Hollywood looks or they are video fine, they come from the right pedigree, they are ambitious and successful, and our family and friends adore them. The only problem is despite all of those admirable attributes, they don't make us happy. Whether there is simply no chemistry, a spiritual disconnect, or our beloved is good at everything else EXCEPT being a good, attentive, and Loving partner, our relationship leaves us feeling alone and uncared for. Our relationship appears warm and cozy; it is the object of the outside world's desire, but our heart is freezing.

When it's cold outside, we usually don't allow the deceptive appearance of the sun to keep us from putting a coat on, turning our heat up in the house, or staying in all together. No matter how warm it looks, we respond to how it feels. Unfortunately this simple principle does not often translate in life. Many of us are in situations right now that look good to everyone else, but they have our spirits shivering, our heart shaking, and our life freezing. Though we usually let "feel" determine how we dress, we often let "looks" determine how we live. When the outside temperature looks warm but feels cold, we cover up. When the outside of our lives look warm but feels cold we cover IT up. Yet, hiding behind bright and sunny looks does not warm up our spirit. So I want to encourage you on this day to commit to making a move, living a life, or choosing a path that keeps your spirit warm.

Take Action

Take your temperature. List the major undertakings in your life along with the major relationships of your life and rate them according to how they make you feel. Use hot, warm, room temperature, cold, and freezing as barometers, with hot being phenomenal and freezing being miserable.

24

Reinvent

Sam Becker wrote an article some time ago in which he explored his thoughts about the 7 biggest business blunders in history. One of those blunders is by the Kodak Company. Kodak was a juggernaut in the camera industry and led in making film, cameras, and eventually disposable cameras. What many people don't know is that Kodak was the first to develop the technology for digital cameras and what would become the cell phone. However, they felt like going down this path was too much of a risk and would change who they knew themselves to be. Becker says, had they followed down this path of evolution, transformation, and reinvention, they could "have become what Apple, Microsoft, and Google are today." Instead, they chose to conduct business as usual and lost business.

Blockbuster Video is responsible for another of the 7 biggest business blunders in history according to Becker. In the early 2000's, Blockbuster had an opportunity to purchase a budding and burgeoning company called Netflix. They opted not to pay $50 million dollars for the company and instead kept much of their energy and efforts in home video rental. Now, Blockbusters are nowhere to be found, and the home video rental industry has been relegated to on demand cable services and Redbox.

Even back in 1870, Alexander Graham Bell offered the patent for the telephone to William Orten for $100,000. Orten was the president of Western Union and had a monopoly on the telegraph. He did not see the possibilities in this new invention and passed up on the telephone.

If Becker is right, then at least three of the top seven business blunders in history all have a common theme. Kodak, Blockbuster, and William Orten's Western Union all share a common denominator in the mistake they made. These three companies saw who they were as being more important than who they could become. As a result they made the critical mistake of not reinventing themselves into something that would have caused them to soar to new levels.

In many different ways and for many different reasons, many of us fall prey to this moribund mindset. We walk through life more intent on conserving what we have and who we have been than on creating who we might turn out to be. It makes sense; we find ourselves most comfortable doing what we know we can do. We feel we are best at being who we have become. We are safest in the relationship we know. Trying something new, doing something different, and reinventing ourselves comes with no guarantee. However, just like the home video died, the telegraph became useless, and 35-millimeter film is gone, your old self will eventually be irrelevant to what the future needs you to be and what you need to be in the future. In the tomorrow of your life, your potential greatness and prospective glory may be dependent on you being someone you have never been, doing something you have never done, and/or trying something you have never tried. The best you is not the old you! It is waiting on you to grow, evolve, and transform. This may be the time to REINVENT.

Take Action

Take time to dream of a new you. List 5 possibilities of how you could reinvent yourself. What ideas may not be serving you as well anymore? Are there any next careers you can imagine for yourself?

25

Get Dressed

So often when I have somewhere to go, or just have the option to get out of the house, I find it difficult to want to get up and get dressed. If somehow I could be teleported from my couch or my bed, then all would be fine, but the getting dressed part can sometimes be a nuisance. I even see this in my son. Many times he will want to leave the house dressed inappropriately because he does not want to change out of the comfort of his house clothes.

One brisk winter day, Bryce and I were preparing to leave the house and I demanded he put on a coat. He complained about the discomfort of having to wear something so bulky as an uncomfortable coat. In the warmth of our house, he had trouble comprehending why he had to wear such a bulky uncomfortable coat when he felt just fine in the house. I explained to Bryce that although he was warm inside, it was freezing outside. With a heated tone and colorful expressions (Christian expressions of course!), I made Bryce understand that we don't get dressed for where we are, we get dressed for where we are going. What we choose to wear, has nothing to do with our present comfort. Getting dressed is a preparation for where we will go, where we will be, and what we will encounter.

Think about it. When we get dressed, we must think about where we are going, and before we even get there, we begin modifying our lives and our behavior for our future. This concept of "getting dressed" is such an important idea for us to internalize in other areas of our lives. We do not wait until we get to our destination to put on our clothes. In fact, getting dressed is an act of preparation in our current location for our future destination.

In one of the books of the Bible considered one of the books of wisdom, we see this same concept at work in the metaphor of the ant; *Proverbs 6:6-8 says, 6) Go to the ant, you lazybones; consider its ways and be wise. 7)Without having any chief officer or ruler, 8) it prepares its food in summer ... (NRSV)* The ant gathers food (act of preparation), during the summer (its current location), so that it can survive the winter (its future destination). Translation: The ant is wise because it "gets dressed."

How many times in life have we chosen to procrastinate on doing the right thing or the best thing until we get "there?" Unfortunately, too often we live our lives and make our choices based on where we are and what we feel right now. We see this in the person who elects to wait on making spiritual commitments until they get their life right. We see this in the student who plans to get better study habits when they begin graduate school, get to college, or begin taking classes in their major. We see this in the person in multiple relationships who decides they will become monogamous when they get in their marriage. In so many cases, we make the decision to put off what would best prepare us for our future because in our present place it is more convenient to stay comfortable.

Finally, whenever we are going somewhere important we "get dressed." I always know when my son is excited to go somewhere because he gets picky about what he wants to wear and he gets motivated to put it on without having to be told. He learned at a young age that when we go somewhere significant, we take more care to get dressed. I believe God wants to take us to important and significant places. Yet, if we are serious about where we are going and if we are excited about our future, then we may have to prepare right where we are in ways that will only make sense when we get where we are going. I know you have somewhere to go .... So put some clothes on!

Take Action

In the next 7 days, do something that you have been putting off that will help set you up for your future.

26

Perseverance

My little sister, whom I Love deeply and dearly, received her Bachelors of Science Degree in Dietetics at Prairie View A&M University this May. It took her seven years. Though I was frustrated with her numerous times along the way, I basked in pride when she graduated because I was struck by the profound amount of perseverance it took her to accomplish this goal. Yes, I could have spent time imagining a million scenarios in which she could have studied harder, focused better, and finished quicker, but another glaring reality stared me in the face. In seven years, she had two thousand five hundred fifty-five opportunities to quit, but she never did! Once she was done with her first four years, there were still one thousand ninety-five opportunities to throw in the towel. However, she pressed on! Now, she can live the rest of her life with an achievement that cannot be taken away.

I mention this because so many of us have decided not to live out a dream, pursue a goal, seize an opportunity, or finish some great feat that we have started because the finish line seems too far from the starting line. So many of us would be lawyers, if it were not for the three years (1,095 days) of law school. So many of us would be doctors, if it were not for the eight years (2,920 days) of medical school and residency. Perseverance is such an important and indispensable part of our ability to succeed. In fact, ask most successful people, and they will tell you that much of their secret was their ability to endure.

I want to encourage someone today to persevere. Find some dream, set some goal, or go after some opportunity, and then take daily steps toward your ambition. Everyday do something, at least one thing, that moves you closer to what you want to do and who you want to be. Those steps add up. Studies suggest that if you spent one hour a day studying anything, in three years you would be an expert in that field. This is evidence of what happens when you persistently stick to anything. Someone might be intimidated by the reality that your aspiration will take five, or even ten, years to accomplish. Yet, if you live for five more years, the only question will be: did you spend those years walking in the direction of your destiny or just wandering directionless? That is why I am so proud of my sister. Clearly, she did not spend each day maximizing each minute of her time, but she never altered her direction. She was persistently pointed toward a degree, and now she has one.

Finally, along with persistence, perseverance takes perspective. You cannot persevere through anything or for anything without a view toward a tomorrow that looks different than your today. In the midst of where you are and what you are going through, you have to be able to see another reality, focus on a better day, and imagine a better possibility. This perceived VISION gives you the fuel to keep moving. If there is no reason to move, no reason to grow, no reason to persist, then there will be no motivation to persevere. All this to say the race is not given to the swift, nor is the battle given to the strong, but to those who endure to the end. Congratulations, Britney! I Love you!

Take Action

Choose something you have always wanted to do but have not. It could be as simple as a hobby or as significant as a career path. Whether you have never started or have dropped your pursuit, pick it up and take small steps toward your goal.

Think

DEEPER

If you grew up in a church anything like the one I grew up in, then you grew up in a church that always wanted you to learn and never wanted you to think. We "learn" information, truths, and beliefs that are already decided. However, when we "think," we investigate and interrogate. For most of us, Christianity has been a journey of being asked to swallow what we are fed and never asking about the ingredients, the recipe, or who created the meal. That is not the Jesus I meet in the gospels.

When asked about the greatest commandment Jesus says that Loving God with all our heart, soul, and mind is one of the two greatest. How do we Love God with our mind? It has to be through thinking. We honor God by taking God, spirituality, and our theology seriously enough to ask questions about them. Questions make us think and rethink. They remind us of what we do not know. They humble us. Think Deeper is not designed to make you agree with me. I do hope it will make you ask questions. I hope it will make you ask questions of yourself, of your ideas of church, religion, and spirituality, and about your ideas of the world where we live.

27

When Healing Hurts

Early in my time as a pastor, one of our members was diagnosed with stomach cancer. As always, it was devastating news. However, as more inquiry was done, doctors realized that it was caught early and it would simply need surgery to expel. The surgery, which consisted of cutting out a small part of the stomach and removing the cancer, was a success. As we sat in the waiting room and listened to the doctor assure us that everything was going to be alright, everyone was relieved.

Now that the surgery was over, the doctor informed the family that their loved one would still be in the hospital another week and then would require three to four weeks of rehabilitation. Four days later they were just to the point where they would allow the consumption of liquids. As I was processing her recovery it dawned on me that all the pain, discomfort, and disability that our member was experiencing was no longer due to the cancer, it was due to the healing. In order to be healed, a stomach had to be cut, a piece of a body part had to be removed, and pain had to be inflicted. This cancer survivor could not eat, was confined to a hospital bed, and was looking at a month's worth of rehabilitation, all in the name of healing. In that moment of reflection I realized the truism that sometimes healing hurts.

It dawned on me that so many times we are not able to remove harmful entities out of our lives because we are not willing to endure the pain that comes with healing. Many of us hold on to ideologies, traditions, actions, and beliefs that are harmful to ourselves and others, simply because we fear the anguish and aching that accompanies their removal. Some of us have relationships with toxic people who are family, friends, or romantic partners, and despite their detriment to our lives we cannot bring ourselves to remove them from our world. Many times we find ourselves waiting for the "right" moment when we can feel "good" about our decision. However, just as cancer does not heal itself, there are some things and people that do not fix themselves. Ultimately, if we are going to be healed, we may have to cut something out, and it may have to hurt.

It would be great if we lived in a world where things that are bad for us would be bad to us, and where decisions for betterment would always feel good. However, the truth is things that we Love can kill us, and pains that we hate can save us. Sometimes we are forced with the decision to either live with a disease that will kill us, or accept a healing process that will hurt us. As we continue to make sense out of a life that occasionally does not offer pain-free choices, I pray that God would give us all the courage and strength to be healed, even when it hurts.

Questions

1. Is there something or someone in your life that you Love that is unhealthy for you?

2. Are there decisions or actions that would help you long term but you are avoiding because they would hurt temporarily?

28
Why I Am Not Saved!

If you have hung around Christians long enough you have met some that have gotten on your nerves … your last nerve! If it's not those who cannot seem to manage a sentence without an "amen," "thank you Jesus," or a "hallelujah," then it may be those who seem to use every opportunity, subject matter, joke, or discussion to interject a scripture quote. I particularly don't care for those who act as Christianity's vanguard and use some moral and doctrinal checklist that is in their head to tell us what and who is or is not "Christian." If you are not finding this amusing right now, then I may be talking about you (don't be too holy for this). Another group that often rubs me the wrong way is those who perpetually herald the fact that they are "saved." These people talk about being "saved" like it is some badge to wear on your chest or some trophy to flaunt in other people's face.

Making salvation a past tense reality that one boasts about not only undermines the virtue of Christian humility (or any humility for that matter), but it also does not properly attend to the reality that we are all people that have habits to break, faults to overcome, and potential to fill. This is why I don't claim salvation in such a manner, nor will you hardly ever hear me say, "I'm saved." I agree with Karl Barth, a theologian who I disagree with on many things, when he talks about salvation as the fulfillment of our being. "Saved" in this line of thinking would mean that I have topped out my capacity, lived completely in my purpose, and delivered to God a person that is all that God has desired and created me to be. This is why I'm not "saved." When we understand salvation as the fulfillment of our being we will soon see that it's not an event, but rather it's a process. Though salvation is defined by a destination, it is lived through a journey.

If by saved you simply mean that God's Love is bigger than my faults, and God's forgiveness has room for all of my failures, then I would have to admit that I am saved. However, I see this more as a statement about the goodness, greatness, and grace of God, and not a declaration about my status. So I prefer to take the emphasis off me, reject myself as subject, remove the "I," and say, "God saves." Yes, God's grace is greater than my guilt. Yes, God's mercy is more powerful than my mischief. Yes, God's compassion looks beyond my carelessness. Still, in the midst of this profound Love, I still find myself headed in the wrong direction, living irresponsibly, and unable to match God's Love with the commitment of my life. How does being "saved" address all that I need to do and become? Consequently, I prefer to spend less time on the pedestal claiming "I'm saved" and more time on the journey with God working on my salvation. Will you journey with me?

Questions

1. What does "saved" mean to you?

2. Do you think there are any parts of salvation that are progressive?

29

Winter Roots

Somewhere in my thirties I found myself gradually trying to develop horticultural skills and to cultivate a green thumb. Yes, though sometimes I didn't believe it myself, I found myself planting flowers, fertilizing grass and shrubs, and watering trees. As I was continuing to educate myself on gardening and plant life, one of the lessons I found most intriguing had to do with the appropriate time to plant new trees. If I am not the only one who was totally clueless to this, then you will be just as surprised as I was to hear that Spring is NOT a good time to plant trees. Rather, planting works best in the fall. This is because the roots of a tree (the most important part of any plant) grow into the ground and are nourished best in the fall and winter due to the perpetual moisture in the Earth's soil.

I witnessed this phenomenon first hand when I purchased and helped plant my very first tree. I planted my first and favorite tree, a Satin Japanese Maple, one fall afternoon. When I planted the tree it looked very scrawny and small, and what little leaves were on it shriveled and died in the winter. I was nervous as I watched my little barren tree suffer through the winter. However, to my amazement in the spring it bloomed bigger, better, and more beautiful. Though the winter was the worst time for the outward appearance of the tree, it was the best time for the roots to grow.

Such is the case with our spiritual lives. I truly believe that our spirits are the roots of our existence. Our growth, health, sanity, and spirituality are dependent on strong roots. Though the spring seasons of our life are filled with blooms and blessings, flowering and flourishing, it is the winter seasons in which our roots grow. It is our ability to endure cold, barren, and seemingly lifeless times that prepares us for our bigger, better, and more beautiful blooms in the spring. If your life is in a spring season right now, take time out to smell the flowers and enjoy the blossoms. But if you are in fall or winter take hold and take courage because your roots are growing!

Questions

1. What are the blooms in your life that began during tough or barren time?

2. What seeds can you plant while you are in a winter season?

30
Why I Love Cherry Blossoms

There is a reason that winter is a metaphor for the roughest patches in our life. Winter is rough! Trees lose leaves, flowers lose blooms, animals lose weight, and sometimes their life, all because of the hardship of winter. Winter storms paralyze cities, close schools, and shut down airports. So often, when we are going through times in life that seem lifeless, we often use winter to describe our reality.

Seasonally, winter lasts from December 21st – March 20th. So, by February we are in the middle of winter. February often has some of the most frigid temperatures and the deadliest storms. However, in Georgia, another thing happens in mid-February – the first blooms of Cherry Blossom Trees. As one whose favorite season is spring and least favorite is winter, I literally long to see the first blooms of the Cherry Blossom trees. No matter how cold, how freezing, or how barren the land is, those blooms remind me that spring is coming.

Cherry Blossoms teach me two very important lessons to hold onto in the winters of my life. God has given us trees that are somehow able to bloom in the middle of winter. When the temperatures are the lowest, the ground is the hardest, and the storms are most abundant, the Cherry Blossom still finds a way flourish and flower. Just as God puts trees in nature that can bloom in the midst of winter, I believe God puts parts in us that can find ways to achieve, accomplish, and thrive when times are at their worst. *We can win in cold and harsh circumstances, and we can bloom in the most difficult circumstances.*

Think Deeper

Secondly, the Cherry Blossom reminds me that winter does not last forever. Whereas some trees bloom after their leaves have come, the Cherry Blossom blooms before the leaves come in the spring. In this way, they are a precursor to what is coming. They tell us that even though we see no leaves; leaves are coming. They let us know that a new season is coming in life and in the tree itself. And if we look close enough, we will find Cherry Blossom like reminders in our life. Winters don't come to last, they come to pass. No matter how barren our lives, or how cold our circumstances during winter, spring comes next. There comes a time when life returns, flowers bloom, and warm weather prevails.

I want to encourage someone today to remember these two lessons. Circumstances do not always have to determine your ability to bloom and blossom. You can flourish in winter. Additionally, winters don't last forever. Spring does come and with it comes life, warmth, and sunshine. Wherever you are, and whatever you may be going through, I pray that God will put Cherry Blossoms in your life.

Questions

1. Identify a time where you grew or flourished in the midst of a difficult time. How did you do it?

2. Where might you be seeing a sign in your life that spring is coming?

31
Why I Don't Like Church

Like myself, my son has very sensitive skin. As a baby and through his toddler years, because of a recent skin irritation he showed after bathing, we had to limit his soap to either Johnson's Baby Wash or Aveeno body wash. As I was asking his pediatrician about the details of this phenomenon, I wanted to know what it was about the cleaning agent in soap that bothered my baby's skin. I was told that it wasn't the actual cleaning ingredients, rather it was all the additives of color and scents that provoked his allergy. It dawned on me today as I was washing towels with unscented Tide Free that Bryce's condition was analogous to my relationship with church.

I have had to consider what it was about church that I didn't like because I am currently in a preaching series entitled, "Why I Go to Church." Now, I know it may sound inauthentic, oxymoronic, and paradoxical for a Pastor to say he doesn't like church, but anyone who knows me well knows this to be true. Oh, I Love Jesus, but I don't like church! If I could get Jesus straight with no chaser I would be fine. However, all the additives in the form of antics, shenanigans, and poorly constructed theologies that color and scent church can be simply repulsive. It bothers me that so many churches big and small have become shrines to wanna-be celebrity preachers who have ecclesiastical entourages, gospel groupies, and faith flunkies. All of a sudden it is beneath men and women to carry their own Bibles, wipe their own sweat, and pour their own water. It hurts me that preachers take the time that can be used to help connect human spirits to a Divine Spirit and use it to convince people to provide luxuries for themselves and their families. It is sad when in many sanctuaries around the country more effort and energy is given toward the prosperity of the Pastor than the poverty of the community. It is troubling when parishioners are apathetic about the progress of their church and the uplift of their community, but are ready to fight over where they want to sit, the color of the carpet, the options on the menu, or the presence or lack thereof of choir robes. Just like those additives that irritate Bryce's skin, church can sometimes make my skin crawl.

To be fair, to say that I don't like church at all would definitely be a misrepresentation and an overgeneralization. So in some sense to discuss "why I don't like church," is to be provocative. However, I am not still a part of church because I necessarily like it. I am here because I believe in it! I believe in the possibilities and the potential of a people who want God to be closer and their world to be better. I believe in God and I believe in Love. Additionally, there are still millions of people who are church goers and church members. I recognize, as a result, I probably do less good if I walk away from it. Since God has a sense of humor I believe God nudged Ayana (that is my made up angel) and said with a grin, "You know, since BaSean doesn't like church, I think I am going to convince him to start one." There you have it! I don't like church, but I Pastor one. Sooo, if you don't like church, but you believe in Love, I'll see you on Sunday.

Questions

1. What do you like or dislike about church?

2. What is your position on attending church, and are you ultimately hurting or helping?

32
Rock Climbing

One of the recreational activities I introduced to my son at an early age is the sport of rock climbing. He began soon after he turned three and did rather well in the beginning. Yet, six months after his first climb a very interesting and intriguing occurrence began to take place. Bryce actually began to become more aware of the challenge and accomplishment of making it to the top of the wall. At first he was just climbing for the pure joy of it without worrying about how far he went. Six months later he was more aware, but he was not quite as good a climber as he was in the beginning. Actually, as his desire to climb increased, his ability to climb decreased. As I was watching him one day, I realized why. When Bryce began, he had a sense of climbing, but was much more interested in the act of climbing itself than whether or not he reached the top. Recently, Bryce's competitive zeal and sense of achievement has heightened and he now attacks the wall with the desire to make it to the top of the wall. However, his zeal is exactly what is hindering his progress. Bryce has formed a habit of looking up for the next rock and reaching without first finding a place to secure his feet. This means he finds himself pulling and holding his entire weight with his arms while his feet sometimes try to gain traction on a flat wall or just dangle all together. Eventually, his little three-year-old hands and arms get too fatigued to continue to pull him up, and exhausted, he begins his descent back down the wall. As he climbs I constantly encourage him to find places for his feet first so that he will have a foundation, but in the end where Bryce wants to be in the future takes more of his attention and effort than where Bryce needs to be to get there. Bryce is so concerned about his future that he forgets to consider his footing and foundation. (Somebody already knows where I am going and should just meet me there.)

Though many of us may not be rock climbers, we often are plagued with Bryce's rock-climbing problems in different areas of our life. So often we want things, want to go places, and want to achieve goals that consume us in such a way that we reach for our destiny without securing ourselves on the proper foundation that will sustain us as we climb. Many of us will reach for a wedding without the foundation of a strong, supportive, Loving, and healthy relationship. Many of us will reach for a prosperous job or career path without the foundation of the purpose and passion that is needed to sustain us through difficult and challenging times. Others of us find ourselves reaching for many desires and destinations without the spiritual foundation that gives us the discipline, peace, and practices that will give us the energy, strength, and stamina that we need. How many spiritual leaders, athletes, celebrities and entertainers have we seen who had the gifts and talents to climb to lofty heights but did not have the spiritual foundation to live a life that would keep them at the top?

When rock climbing, Bryce needs his arms and hands to reach, but he needs his legs and feet to climb. Great rock climbers know the art of securing their footing. Great life climbers know the importance of securing their foundation. When life climbing, our gifts and talents can take us high, but without the foundation of a secure and stable spirit we will never be able to sustain our climb or climb to our highest point. Without a firm spiritual foundation, at some point, our arm strength will give up and our hands will get fatigued. We simply cannot afford to allow where we want to be in the future, to eclipse where we need to be in the present to reach our destiny and stay there. As you reach for your future and climb toward your destiny, don't forget to secure the spiritual foundation that you will need to reach the top.

Questions

1. When or where in your life do you find yourself reaching too fast without securing your foundation?

2. What are the dreams for your life that could slip away if you do not have a secure foundation?

3. What does a secure foundation look like for you?

33
Why I Boycotted the NFL

I Love football. No really, I LOVE football. I played it through college, coached it as a parent, and I have watched it for my whole life. I still dream about playing. In my thirties and through my early forties I have probably played kickball with the energy, drive, and passion that I do because it fills the void left by my Love of playing football. Anyone who knows me knows that the idea of boycotting the NFL was something that was a colossal challenge for me. I Love football, but for the season of 2017, I refused to watch because Colin Kaepernick did not get signed to a team.

I am boycotting because I supported Colin Kaepernick's protest during the National Anthem. In the season of 2016, Colin Kaepernick sat out and took a knee during the national anthem. When challenged about his decision he explained that he would not celebrate the moment of the national anthem while America did not live out the values of equality and justice that are pillars of its constitutional and moral existence. Many believed and still believe this was disrespectful to the flag, the country, veterans, and soldiers. I believed and still believe it demonstrated a deeper belief and Love for the best hopes of this country, than those who are more concerned with symbols than substance. If America or Americans are not living the flag, then we should respect those who won't stand for it.

I boycotted because NFL owners have shown that black people standing erect during the national anthem is more important than black people lying dead in the streets. In short, every owner, player, fan, and casual observer had essentially two choices once Kaepernick gave voice to the systemic oppression and fatal police brutality experienced by black and brown people in this country. They could prioritize a symbol and a song, or they could prioritize the actual lives of the "Americans" the symbols and songs are about. With the exception of Stephen Ross of the Miami Dolphins, who at least supported his players protesting, there was little vocal and public support from the National Football League for the black people that make up 70% of its players.

I boycotted the NFL owners because I did not want the voices of white supremacy to be louder than the voices of progress, equality, and Love. Many were convinced this was not a black issue but a business issue. The NFL owners were worried about the distraction and backlash they would have received if they signed Colin Kaepernick. Even if this was true, it was true because there were voices out there who were against Kaepernick and his protest. There were and still are voices who are willing to boycott the NFL or pull their sponsorship over a song (the National anthem) and a symbol (the standing for the flag). The idea that one's posture during the singing of a song that is historically racist (read the lyrics of the whole song) is more important than the bullet ridden bodies of black and brown men, women, and BOYS on the street is deeply racist. So, if there were voices so inspired by symbols that they would boycott the NFL, I will always be inspired enough by black life and protest to speak up. If there were voices willing to stand up against Colin, I chose to be a voice standing for and with him and the cause of unarmed black people being unjustly killed while their killers are being unjustly under-prosecuted.

I almost chose to not boycott. I almost chose to prioritize my being entertained by a game over my standing for a just cause. At some point it hit me that I was allowing my thirst for entertainment to reign more powerful than my thirst for justice. In the end, I wanted to believe that I was bigger than that, and people's lives are more important than that. I mean here Colin Kaepernick was willing to risk money, sponsorships, and his job to stand in solidarity with people he actually didn't even know. Surely, I could give up my choice of entertainment for a season. Ultimately, as a Christian, I claim to follow someone who was murdered, in part, because he stood with the least, the lost, the last, the left out, and the left behind. Standing for Kaepernick, who was kneeling for vulnerable lives, didn't come close to costing me my life. It only cost me my choice of entertainment. Innocent lives had to be worth at least that.

I Love football, but I chose to not watch an entire season in support of Colin Kaepernick. For many, one simple season not watching the NFL was too much. For me, I wonder if my one simple season of boycotting was not enough.

Questions

1. What are the issues or injustices that you believe are worth taking a stand?

2. Have you ever boycotted or protested anything? Why or why not?

3. Have you ever been moved to take a social stand against something you Loved for something you Loved more?

34
In the Weeds

Whether you know it or not, all of us have experienced the feeling of being "in the weeds." Once, I was literally in the weeds as I was attending to a small flower bed that our church had planted where we worship. Some time ago we planted a tree, several shrubs, Azalea's, ornamental grass, and several flowers for our church. In order to properly care for the plants, we added our own soil and soil conditioner to feed and nurture the roots for all the new vegetation we planted. Interestingly enough, I soon found out the soil not only fostered the growth of what we wanted to grow, but it also fueled things we did not want to grow. A month later weeds had grown faster and taller than the flowers we originally planted. I wish I could tell you that those weeds came out of nowhere and all of a sudden I was shocked that they had taken over the flower bed. However, the truth is I noticed when they first sprouted and did nothing. Oh, I noted to myself that they would be a problem, but I put off handling it for another day. Well, a day went to days, days turned to weeks, and before I knew it I had a flower bed full of the greenest, healthiest, most vibrant … WEEDS.

As I was on my knees pulling weed after weed hoping that the roots of the weeds had not connected to the roots of the flowers, I began to reflect on the life lesson that I was learning. On one hand we had provided the flowers and ornamental grass everything they needed to bloom and blossom into a beautifully landscaped presentation. On the other hand the same fertilizer, soil, and conditioner that helped the things we wanted to prosper also aided things we did not want to prosper. In fact it assisted the very thing that could have suffocated our original design. The same context and conditions that produced flowers also provided weeds. I wish life and landscaping made it easy for the things that we want to bloom to grow without the things that we don't want to rise as well. However just like that flower bed, when great things bloom and blossom in our lives they are almost always accompanied by weeds. Success is accompanied by stress, jealousy, and haters. Fame is accompanied by temptations and seductions. Money is accompanied by greed, meaninglessness and artificial friendships. Churches are accompanied by holy hypocrites, cliques, and power struggles. Even our country exemplifies how great ideas like democracy, entrepreneurism, and freedom can be accompanied by imperialism, genocide, slavery, sexism, and homophobia.

Nevertheless, those weeds did not have to overtake our flowers, and our weeds don't have to consume and conquer our lives. I had the opportunity to pick, pull, or chop those weeds out as soon as I saw them, but the beauty of the flowers distracted me from the urgency of the weeds. We allow this to happen all the time in our relationships, our society, our careers, and our personal lives. We look at what is good, and though we see some budding problems and predicaments, we put off addressing the weeds in our lives in order to continue smelling the flowers in our lives. This procrastination soon finds us covered and even conquered by weeds and before we know it life's demands become too much for our supply and we suffocate. So make up your mind today that no matter how beautiful the flowers are in your life, you will also pay attention to the weeds.

Questions

1. What are some great things in your life that brought about the unintended growth of weeds?

2. How do you attend to the weeds in your life?

3. Is there anything in your life so beautiful that it is distracting you from the weeds that may be growing?

35

Privilege

She can preach for a woman." It is something that has never been said about me and I have been preaching for over 30 years. I am a man. I know, "Duh!" right? However, what that means is, whenever I stand in front of a new congregation, I don't have to worry about my speaking abilities being doubted because of my gender. In fact, because most people have grown up hearing men give sermons, they develop an expectation and often even develop a preference for men to preach. This is not because there have not been men that have given bad speeches or preached horrible sermons. It is because most of us have seen men preach so much that men and preaching go hand in hand. Most people who grew up in church worshipped under a male pastor, so most (if not all) sermons many have heard growing up were preached by men, in some cases, exclusively men. Pastoring and preaching is and has been a male dominated field.

Since people are used to seeing men preaching, my being a man never serves as a barrier to me connecting to an audience. There may be other factors that serve as a challenge: my height, my color, my deep Texas drawl. But I have never had to worry about an audience thinking I am too masculine to be an effective preacher. This benefit of the doubt my being a man affords me is a privilege. I did not earn it by any effort of mine, nor did I merit it by any particular striving or speaking talent. It is given to me by the society and culture where I live. It is a privilege … a male privilege. I don't get to turn it off or opt out. I don't get to say no or deny the advantages I am given by virtue of being a man. Every time I stand to preach as a man, I can rest assured my masculinity will not be a problem whether I like it or not. Needless to say, my sisters in ministry are not afforded the same privilege, and no matter how much I may personally be in solidarity with my sisters, I still cannot shred my personal privilege as a man.

In this highly-racialized climate we live in today, we hear a lot about "white privilege." Often, I have heard my white brothers and sisters talk about white privilege as something they can choose to divest themselves from. Some of my friends and acquaintances have articulated this idea that they can turn white privilege on or off in their own personal world. Yet, just like I cannot earn or divest myself of my male privilege, white people cannot choose or decline white privilege. Just like male privilege is built on a long history of male domination, white privilege is built on the legacy of white domination in America. We cannot rid ourselves of the biased privileges a society steeped in discrimination afford us. Privilege is bigger than our personal choices. Privilege is found in how the masses have been trained to look at us, judge us, and give us the benefit of the doubt. We don't get to say no to privilege. Yet we can use our privilege. We can use it to further perpetuate male domination, white supremacy, heterosexism, patriarchy, and other forms of oppression. On the other hand, we can use our privilege to resist the very domination that serves as its foundation. Since some of the "gifts" of privilege are voice and visibility, we can use our voices and visibility to educate, resist, own, and acknowledge how domination makes an oppressive, provincial, and limited world. In short, instead of wasting time denying that privilege exists in our world, or in our behavior, the best thing we can do with our privilege is to own it and use it ... for good.

Think Deeper

Questions

1. Are you able to identify a place(s) in your life where you have or live in privilege?

2. Have you ever used your privilege to be in solidarity with those who are less privileged than you?

36
Have a "MARY" Christmas

Have you ever thought about what Christmas was like for Mary? After going through 9 months of a socially embarrassing and unexpected teenage pregnancy she finds herself in the discomfort of travel on dirt roads. She has the luxury of switching from walking to riding on a top of the line DONKEY, and somewhere in the midst she begins experiencing labor pains. Then, instead of going to a comfortable labor room or a deluxe suite at a nearby hotel, she is left to suffer through delivery between the foul stench of animals and the nagging pricks of hay on her back.

If the immediate discomforts of pregnancy in the 1st century, labor on the road, and delivery in a barn were not enough, can you imagine the nerves and fears of an unwed teenage mother in the highly judgmental environment of purity focused Judaism? If you cannot imagine the environment just think of the average "purity-and-holiness" driven Christian church today. Mary was surrounded by scowls of disapproval, talking-behind-her-back peers, and forced to live a life of socio-religious marginalization. Parents didn't want their daughters to be Mary's friend, church members bad mouthed her in their homes, she was unable to eat and socialize with "good" Jews, and in every religious service or ritual she observed she could not worship with the pure. Yeah, being called to be God's mom was not all it was cracked up to be.

The point I am making is that the first Christmas did not come without a serious cost and a profound sacrifice from someone - Mary. Great things, grand moments, and miraculous events rarely occur without someone who is willing to give up some things and endure personal discomfort for the sake of a preferred future and a better world. Yes, Christmas is the celebration of the gift God gave the world in the birth of Jesus. Yet the means of God's work is the life of a bright eyed young teenage woman whose life would never be the same because of her willingness to be used by God. I believe Christmas is a grander version of how God works daily in the world. God takes human willingness to be used by God and blesses us with acts, moments, and events that give us pieces of the Divine. In this sense, every day is an opportunity for Christmas when we allow ourselves to let God work through us.

During Christmas season, many people wish us a Merry Christmas. The hope is that you will be consumed with Christmas spirit, enjoy the company of family and friends, and be blessed by the giving and receiving of gifts. Indeed this is a beautiful sentiment. However, for us to have a "Merry" in Christmas today there had to be a Mary for Christmas years ago. Christmas needs a Mary who will be an instrument for God's work and movement in the world. Christmas needs a Mary who will sacrifice for other people and future moments. So, I want to wish something weightier and greater for your life this Christmas – the opportunity to be God's Mary. While many will wish you a "Merry Christmas," for your next Christmas season, I want to wish you a Mary Christmas!

Questions

1. How are you allowing God to work through you for some greater good?

2. Are there aspects of Mary's life that you have never considered?

37
"YES WE DID!"

On November 4, 2008, "Yes We Can" turned into "Yes We Did". Seemingly out of nowhere a man, who by virtue of his race, may have been excluded from countless institutions and organizations in America some fifty years ago, would have been legally barred from first class citizenship in America one hundred years ago, and could have been enslaved in America one hundred and fifty years ago, became the leader of America. Wow!!!

Obama ran his campaign on the campaign slogan, "Yes We Can." When we reflect on this historic election and eight years of a historic presidency, I often think about whom exactly this "we" includes. As an African-American man, it is tempting to simply hail the record turnout of black voters who showed up everywhere or to outline the long historical struggles of black leaders who have fought, bled, and died so that life could be better for their progeny. I mean who didn't get the text that swept across the landscape of Black History and into future by announcing, "Harriet went under, so that Rosa could sit, so that Martin could march, so that Obama could win, so that our children can fly!" There is no doubt that "we" includes enslaved Africans, freedom fighters, ordinary black people throughout our history in America, civil rights activists, black politicians, black preachers, black educators, black athletes, black entertainers, and black business people. "Yes We Did."

Yet what makes me even happier as a black man in America is that this accomplishment by a fellow black man cannot exclusively be owned by black people. As almost every achievement for black people in America, there is some shared multicultural and multiracial responsibility. The "we" includes my beautiful brown brothers and sisters of Latino history and heritage who lent some 67% of their vote to Obama. The "we" includes my progressive white brothers and sisters who comprised 61% of the votes cast for Obama. In the end, there were people of all kinds of ancestry, gender, sexual orientation, class, and religious affiliation that put aside the status quo of the past 43 white male presidents, fought past racism and white supremacy, and believed that a person could be judged, trusted, and believed in as a result of his work ethic, ideas, and achievements. "Yes We Did."

Believe it or not, the "we" even includes people that we might never suspect. Though I am fervently and frequently against most of their politics, the appointments of Clarence Thomas, Condoleezza Rice, and Colin Powell by the "Bushes" went a long way in transforming the psyche of many white Americans in relation to their ability to grasp black people in political leadership. So, for whatever part George Bush Sr. and George Bush Jr. may have unintentionally had in the election of Barack Obama, I say: "Yes We Did!"

I could go on and on, but I'll leave you alone and encourage you to read as much commentary as you can on this historic happening. However, I leave you with one remaining thought. One of the beauties of this election, and the multidimensional "we" that combined to ensure an Obama victory, is that in one swoop we got a realistic taste of what American Democracy, Martin Luther King's beloved community, and Jesus' community of God, can really look like. "Yes We Did!!!!!"

Questions

1. How did you experience the election of Barack Obama in 2008?

2. What individuals or groups do you believe made up the "we" of Obama's campaign slogan?

38
Bless You For What?

All of us in some shape, form, or fashion want to be blessed! If we took inventory of our last prayer, I am sure at some point we asked God to bless our family, bless our finances, bless our relationship(s), bless our country, and/ or bless our children. If we have prayed the prayer of Jabez (asking God to increase our territory), asked for "favor," or requested "the anointing," then in short we were asking God for a blessing. Even the most holiest and altruistic among us may ask for wisdom, self-discipline, or justice, but this still translates into asking God for a blessing. Asking God to move, manipulate and/or maneuver us or our situation, eventually adds up to asking God to bless us.

Yet, have you ever thought about what your answer would be if God stopped you in the middle of your prayer and asked, "Bless you for what?" "For what reason do you want to be blessed?" "What do you want to do with your blessing?" "Will it matter to Me or the world if I give you this blessing?" What if God kneeled beside you at your bedside or sat in the passenger seat of your car while you were driving and asked, "Why do you want more money?" "What is the purpose of a bigger house?" "Why do you want more power or fame?" In short, what if God asked you, "What's in it for Me?"

The point I am making is that many of us pray to a God who we expect to be a Grand Personal Assistant that exists for our benefit and our blessings. In a spiritual age where we are assured that we can "name it and claim it" and "believe it and receive it," we are slowly being lured to a spirituality that is 99% about us. In short, we have become the center of our own universe and

God is just a means to execute our plans, provide our pleasures, and assure our prosperity. When all our preaching is about how God can make our life better and richer, and all our praising is in hopes that the "blessings will come down," we reduce religion, and God for that matter, to our very own whims and wishes.

I know that this sounds harsh, but just stop and think for a minute. When is the last time you have really, I mean really, been consumed with a cause that is beyond your life and higher than your existence? Don't move on! Really think about that question!

Blessings are great and all of us want them. However, to see yourself as simply the receptacle of blessings is to lower your stature, diminish your greatness, and miss the point. When God gives the famous "blessing of Abraham," we should listen carefully to what God says. "I will make you into a great nation and I will bless you: I will make your name great and you will be a blessing." I firmly believe we are all meant to be great, but greatness comes in being a blessing not simply getting one. So, the next time you pray and ask God to bless you (and you will), be prepared to answer God, if God stops you and asks, "Bless you for what?"

Questions

1. Do you find your prayers consumed with yourself and your desires for blessings?

2. Do you pray that your blessings will impact something or someone beyond you?

39

Can We Critique Obama?

Anyone who is deeply involved in the inner leadership culture of Fellowship of Love Church, will tell you that it is a deeply critical culture. Though it is constructively critical, it is critical nonetheless. This has not always been the case. Just like all cultures, the defining traits, characteristics, values, and practices are in part taught, nurtured, and groomed. Such is the case with the constructively critical nature of our church culture. When we first began, it was extremely difficult for me to get our Executive Team to feel comfortable critiquing my sermons. The members of our team had grown up in cultures where the Pastor was to be revered and respected, thus, offering public critique was seen as disloyal and disruptive. Week after week I would ask for criticisms of my preaching and week after week I was given blank stares and shoulder shrugs expressing, "I thought it was good." Finally, one day I had to say something that amounted to this: "I am not a perfect preacher, and I want to be a better preacher. Unless you expect for me to unconsciously slip into becoming better, I need you to tell me when you think I am bad or wrong, and I will have to trust that you are telling me what you think is best. If not, the kind of support you are giving me will cripple my growth."

During the presidency of Barack Obama a familiar debate resurfaced about whether black people should publicly critique other black people. One place this debate crystallized was when there was discussion about Obama being selected for the Nobel Peace Prize. Before his selection, the mere possibility of him winning found me torn between excitement and fear. Though there were some valid arguments for other candidates and against Obama, I did understand and supported his selection for the Nobel Peace Prize. In a world where many countries had closed their mouths and plugged their ears to international conversation about diplomacy, global moral responsibility, and how to live together peacefully, it was an achievement to open doors of conversation that had previously been closed. In a nihilistic world where many people have given up on America as anything but a rich, greedy, and imperialistic gangster and given up on the possibility of world peace, it was an accomplishment to give international hope about the possibility of world peace. This incalculable achievement and invaluable accomplishment places Obama in the conversation of Nobel Peace Prize winner. Yet, in spite of my personal view, I did not consider critique of Obama on this matter or others as only a sign of disloyalty, lack of patriotism, or "haterism" as many supporters of Obama did.

There were valid concerns about giving the Commander in Chief of the United States an award for peace while violent and suspect military operations happened all around the globe. I was fearful that supporters of Obama were taking the same attitude and disposition that the executive team at Fellowship of Love took towards my preaching. If we Love Obama, and all he represents, we cannot view critique of Obama as disloyal and disruptive. We also cannot disregard any and every one's objections and criticisms of Obama as propaganda from those who just don't like the fact that he was our president. As great a president as Barack Obama was, I hope we can all agree that he was not and will not be perfect. In the midst of imperfection, Christian Love must always want the best from and in everyone. Therefore, Barack Obama needed our support and Love, even when that Love came in the form of constructive criticism. If we are afraid to critique Obama, or anyone else we find heroic, then we will be resolved to cripple them. So, can we critique Obama? I believe we have to …

Questions

1. If you were a supporter of Barack Obama, was there any point that you were critical of him?

2. Identify someone who you look up to socially, politically, spiritually, or personally. Where are they wrong, and where can they be better?

3. Do you believe critique is a necessary component of Loving someone?

40

Spiritual Jazz

I have previously detailed why I like Hip-Hop Culture and how I believe that in some ways it serves as a metaphorical paradigm for how we can live more spiritually. However, jazz is another musical genre that serves as a means to provoke thinking about how we can make sense out of life and live life more meaningfully.

One of the characteristics that makes jazz so notable and unique is its penchant for improvisation. While classical music may be unpredictable as one listens, it is set to a musical score which is fixed and takes the musician from beginning to end. From the first note to the last, it takes us on a journey with highs and lows, crescendos and decrescendos. On the other hand, rap, rhythm and blues, and even most rock is marked by a circular beat with a lyrical formula of verse, hook, verse, hook, with a bridge here or there. Of course, this is an extreme over simplification of these genres, but it does outline them generally. Yet jazz, at its best is a musical movement that improvises and moves according to feel, mood, and response to other musicians.

Many of us attempt to make our lives "classical" by making plans, writing scripts for ourselves, or determining where we will be and when we will get there. Yet, we soon find out that the forces in the world do not always cater to our desires or our designs. Life offers us curve balls, detours, roadblocks, and obstacles that place us in situations and circumstances that we never imagine. I mean how many of us growing up just knew that life would be as simple as going to college, getting married, having kids, working until retirement, and living happily ever after? Yet after heartbreak, children, career changes, fall outs with friends, family, and/or lovers, or any host of other occurrences we are working a job our college education did not prepare us for, with or without a person we never imagined, or living a lifestyle that did not fit the high expectations of our childhood.

Others of us are living "rhythm and blues" lives that are full of routine and regimen that find the beat of our lives moving in the same daily, weekly, or monthly circles. Whatever the case, as we continue to pray for progress in our lives, we may need to ask God to help make us spiritual jazz musicians. We should petition God, TODAY, to give us the audacity to stop the lackadaisical loops, break the myopic molds, and interrupt the regular routines that hold us hostage and keep us from flying. When things change around our lives, we need God to help us change notes in our lives, while still being able to make beautiful music out of our lives.

The good news is that as we peruse the profound pages of the Bible we find a God just like this. Whether it is the slavery of Joseph, the fall of Sampson, the lustful greed of David, the trials of Hagar, the unwanted pregnancy of Mary, the betrayal by Judas, or the crucifixion of Jesus, God continually shows the improvisational skills to turn something out of nothing, make blessings from burdens, and bring life out of death. So, jazz up your life and don't live a life of stagnation when you have a God of improvisation.

Questions

1. What are some of the "regular routines" of your life that hold you hostage?

2. How could you live a more improvisational life?

41

Christmas...Christians...Refugees

In November of 2015, a four-year Syrian crisis hit home in the United States in a more visible way than ever before. Then President Barack Obama laid out a plan to resettle some 10,000 Syrian refugees fleeing political strife and oppression. Governors all across the United States, including the State of Georgia where I live and the State of Texas where I was reared, began protesting the Federal Government's decision to allow Syrian refugees into the United States. As I began to see the polls, hear the commentary, and read the Facebook comments, my heart sank as citizens and more importantly Christians showed vehement hostility and little empathy to the men, women, and children of Syria who were literally running for their lives.

Christians who serve, follow, and even worship perhaps the most famous refugee in history, had either forgotten or not paid close attention to a story that many were about to begin celebrating as we were entering the Christmas season. Clearly we had forgotten that almost as soon as Jesus was born, the leader of an oppressive military regime was hunting for his life. That's right! After the wise men would not participate in Herod's plot to capture and kill Jesus, he put out an order to kill all the children in and around Bethlehem who were two years old or under. This is all recorded in the book of Matthew's account detailing the beginning of the life of Jesus. Mary, Joseph, and Jesus fled to Africa as refugees to escape the death threat of Herod. Someone had to be compassionate enough to accept them. Jesus' survival depended on Africans being Loving enough to give refuge to a foreigner whose life was in danger.

Some two thousand years later, Americans, who have built a faith around a refugee from Bethlehem, could not find the same Love in their heart as Syrian refugees scrambled to find safe haven from the violence of Civil War and the threat of the Islamic State in Iraq and Syria (ISIS). Even if we could not learn from our faith, we should at least have taken heed of the facts. According to the reports of Meet the Press, from 9/11 to 2015, 785,000 refugees were admitted in America. Out of those hundreds of thousands, only about a dozen were arrested or removed due to terrorist concerns. This is about .0015% of refugees. However, none of those who have been removed or arrested were Syrian.

People of faith always have a responsibility to discern what their faith asks of them in any given political climate. Whenever we consider the miracle, magic, and majesty of Christmas, I hope those of us who Love Christ, will remember the kind of Love it took to keep Christ alive. I don't know if those Africans who took in Mary, Joseph, and their child knew the historical impact of what they were doing. I imagine they did not. That's what makes it beautiful. They simply chose to Love and a man who would change the religious landscape of the world was saved. They chose to Love, and 2000 years later my life was altered by that baby boy from Bethlehem. They … simply…. chose … to …. LOVE! And when we choose to Love, we never know what God might do.

Questions

1. Have you ever considered that Christianity is in some ways indebted to people who chose to Love and be open to refugees?

2. Does remembering that Jesus was a refugee give you a different view of present-day refugees?

42

Obama, Flaming Sharks, and Exceptionalism

One of the most fulfilling victories of my life happened to me while coaching my son's 7-8-year old flag football team, "The Flaming Sharks." When I coach, I use a swift democratic process to allow the children to name their team, and it can go from familiar names like "The Heat" and "The 49ers" to quite interesting names like "The Thrusting Panthers" (that is a real name of a former team I have coached). This particular season we were "The Flaming Sharks."

As we entered the season, what was supposed to be a league of 7-8-year olds turned into a league of 7-9-year olds. This concerned me. I was especially apprehensive because my team of mostly 7-year olds, had to face a team of mostly 9-year olds twice during the season. More importantly, I believed it was unfair to the younger teams filled with many 7-year olds to place them in competition against 9-year olds. The various developmental levels of children are such that this was comparable to a college team playing in a league full of high school teams. The activist in me called the director in the league and protested the blatant unfairness of this arrangement. These children had been set at a disadvantage by a system that allowed them to compete in unfair conditions. I wrote the director and spoke to him by phone about how it could possibly be deflating and intimidating to have second graders competing against fourth graders. Yet none of my complaints about the blatant unfairness of this league led to change.

Of course our first game was against the 9-year olds, and of course we lost handily. The cherry on top was that we had to play them the last game of the season so that we could end our season as we began. As we improved during the year, I began to strategize, plan, and even install a couple of trick plays in an attempt to at least make us competitive for our last game. As luck would have it, our last game got postponed due to rain, and we were able to schedule an extra practice. By the time we played the game, we had to play a now undefeated and relatively untested mostly 9-year old team. My 7-year olds played the game of their lives, and when the dust had settled we pulled out a victory with a score of 20-14.

Though I was thrilled in the beginning, I began to have great reservations about what had just happened. I was afraid that somehow it would now become easy for the director to use our victory to continue placing seven 7-year olds in unfair conditions. I knew deep down that despite our success, it would be unfair to expect that 7-year olds could regularly beat or even compete against 9-year olds. I didn't want the league to regularly place second grade children against fourth grade children and then point to us to tell them to practice hard, try hard, and they could beat fourth graders just like we did. I had a couple of very exceptional 7-year old athletes who played an exceptional game and beat exceptionally long odds. However, this exceptional group of kids was just that, the exception.

This is the same problem many progressive leaders and thinkers had with President Obama's attempt to help young black men through his My Brother's Keeper program in the year 2014. This program was a well-intended attempt to mentor and motivate young men of color by placing examples of successful black men in their lives. As needed as mentorship is, young black and particularly poor black men still have conditions that are bigger than them that make winning a long shot and the game of life inequitable. Placing exceptional black men in a room and pointing to them as an example of what "any black" man can do misses the point of how poverty, systemic racism, and callous education policies make winning on any grand scale a manifestation of exceptionalism. To be sure, I am a huge fan of mentoring. I am not a huge fan of people with the power to change foundational rules solely relying on mentoring to fight systemic inequities.

Young black leaders and young black men are in the same dilemma I found myself in that fall season. No matter how unfair it may have been, the season did happen and the games had to be played. Even in unfair conditions, we had to practice, prepare, and plan to be competitive. Likewise, black people must educate ourselves, work hard, and strive to make our place in the world because no matter how unfair, life goes on. However, if I was the director of the league, I would have made a policy that would not place 7-year olds in conditions that I know are not fair to them. As I see it, one of the primary responsibilities of a director is to make rules that create a fair playing field. I would not have simply gathered coaches and had a clinic on how to coach 7-year olds to victory over 9-year olds. The truth is, if you do not have the exceptional above average athletes I had, your coaching matters very little. Just like 7-year olds have the unfair disadvantage of physical immaturity, less highly developed speed, agility, and aggression, and a lower competitive IQ, poor black young men (and women for that matter) have the disadvantage of less resources, fewer examples, a shorter history of equal freedom and opportunities, policies that are indifferent to their welfare, and curriculums that are often indifferent to their learning styles.

President Obama had an opportunity to address the plight of young black men by striving to change the conditions of the league. Instead he led a cry to help young black men try harder, practice harder, and try to win whatever their conditions. Obama said:

"You will have to reject the cynicism that says the circumstances of your birth or society lingering injustices necessarily define you and your future… It will take courage, but you will have to tune out the naysayers who say if the deck is stacked against you, you might as well just give up or settle into the stereotype."

Obama's speech to young black men was what any coach who did not have the power to change the league should say to his team. It echoes what I told my 7-year olds as they faced a 9-year old team. Here is the problem, Obama was not the coach of a team in a league, he was the director of the league. People who have power, influence power, or vote for those in power, always have a responsibility to focus on the rules that make fair play for all. So, while I totally support Obama's charge to young black men and his plea for people to help them win; I wanted Obama, just as I want all those in power, to do the same thing that I wanted the director of that flag football league to do… CHANGE THE LEAGUE!!

Questions

1. Can you identify instances where success is the exception?

2. Have you ever been a part of an unfair system? What was the system and why was it unfair?

43

Beyonce, Black Panthers, and Black Love

Super Bowl 51 was so memorable to me for many reasons. Amidst the crowning of the Denver Broncos as Super Bowl Champions, and Von Miller (my homeboy from DeSoto, Tx who went to my high school, DeSoto "U" … ok, I am sorry; I digress) as MVP, there was another significant moment that took place that weekend. On the Saturday before the Super Bowl, Beyonce dropped a video, "Formation," with an obvious ode to her black people, black Love, and Black justice. In one video, she remembered Hurricane Katrina, embraced her black roots and black aesthetic features, and fell in line with the Black Lives Matter movement through the image of a young black boy in a hoodie dancing in the midst of a line of white police officers with graffiti in the background saying "stop shooting us." Sunday, Beyonce followed up the formation video with a Super Bowl halftime performance where she dressed in all Black and had all female dancers dressed like Black Panthers in the same "X" formation as parts of her video.

Of course, Beyonce has received tons of criticism for making her performance a political act and for paying homage to the Black Panther Party. Of course, this criticism is filled with the hypocrisy that has assailed Black people and Black Love throughout history in America. Every major sporting event in America begins as a political act. What do you think is happening when the Star Spangled Banner is sung? When people are asked to stand up, take off their hats and helmets, and put their hands over their hearts while the National Anthem is sung, this IS political. When military jets fly over the stadium and military men and women are peppered on the field throughout the pregame, this IS political. Yet, few have ever expressed issue with these political acts. In fact Colin Kaepernick lost a career and the NFL has lost fans over these political moments. Yet, Beyonce celebrates a Black Panther Party which was formed to combat this country at it's ugliest, most unjust, and most unfair and somehow American football fans decided they would rather not be political. Beyonce's performance essentially asserted, "If we can celebrate the country before the game, we can celebrate people who have confronted this country and pushed it to be better in the middle of the game."

Of course, for some, the problem was not necessarily the political act but rather the political people (i.e. The Black Panther Party) and their stance that violence was a legitimate and necessary means to gain justice for Black people. I am amazed at how "Americans" can selectively support and oppose violence. When America wanted freedom from British rule, they used violence. I don't see these critics boycotting The Fourth of July. When America colonized and expanded "American" territory from sea to shining sea, they used violence to kill and displace Native Americans. America grew as a world power largely on the backs of a free labor economic system called slavery. Need I remind us that slavery was barbarically violent? Nevertheless, when a group organized to protect blacks who were unjustly abused physically, psychologically, culturally, economically, legally, and politically, they were somehow wrong. When a Black Panther Party appeals to the same violence that formed and built this country they are out of line. Black Panther hate and the barrage of criticism of Beyonce simply lays bare the historical ignorance and racism (external and internal) of a people in a country that has violently climbed its way to the top and yet reserves the right of violence to the American Empire. Even if America's actual and historical violence exponentially exceeds a Black Panther Party whose commitment to violence was far more philosophical than actual, critics would still turn a blind eye to American history and try to poke out the eye of anyone who would appreciate people standing up for Black people.

So I will forever be grateful to Beyonce for her Super Bowl performance. I know that her musical symbolism does not have the critical depths and substance to make a comprehensive revolution for the underserved and unjustly treated in America. I know Beyonce is still largely immersed in capitalism, consumerism, and materialism. However, in the world of Black preachers that I am a part of, where so many preachers are refusing to vocally and/or visibly stand up for black justice, black people, and black Love, I am glad somebody is Loving black people enough to parade our struggle in front of the masses. So, I say "Thank You!" to Beyonce for taking the risk to Love Black people politically and publicly. Maybe now that Beyonce has made a video she might free some black pulpits to declare, "Black Lives Matter!"

Questions

1. What are your thoughts about the Black Panther Party?

2. Have you ever researched the history and contributions of the Black Panther Party?

3. Do you see a need for "Black" Love?

44

Fashion, Racism, and Jesus

While listening to an Atlanta morning show one morning in 2010, the issue of Essence Magazine hiring a white fashion director surfaced. Essence editor Angela Burt-Murray hired Elliana Placas (a white woman) and was heavily criticized by former Essence fashion editor and founding fashion director of Vibe magazine, Michaela Angela Davis. The critique of Davis argues that since "the fashion industry is not diverse – it is an elite, closed world and there is very little place for black women," then by closing yet another door to a black woman Essence made a lamentable decision. She further contends, since Essence makes black women a part of their brand and DNA, that this should be reflected in its top-level hiring practices.

Each radio personality quickly dismissed Davis' point by caricaturing her as a disgruntled former employee and an embodiment of reverse racism. Now on one hand, I must admit that I have not had enough time to really sort out exactly where I stand on this particular issue and occurrence. Nevertheless, I am saddened by those who do not feel the force of Davis' point, even if in the end they disagree (or don't feel it holds enough weight to advocate changing Essence's decision). More importantly, I am troubled by the shallow and thinly thought argument that it is reverse racism when a black woman contends that a magazine, that claims prioritizing black women is a part of its mission, should not hire a white woman as a fashion director.

Reverse racism is so often misused because of a misunderstanding of racism itself and its distinction from discrimination or race bias. It is not helpful to reduce racism to anyone's bias for their race or against another race. Racism more comprehensively details a system, and participation in such a system, that historically, methodically, and presently contributes to abuse and subjugation of a race of people. Racism is about the deep interconnections of PRESENCE and POWER. Take fashion for instance. When we look across the landscape of the fashion industry in America, whose presence have we historically seen in fashion and in positions of power? Go to the fashion section in Barnes and Noble and in a bookstore in the airport, scan the magazine cover pages, and thumb through the pages and locate the editors, directors, and executives. Is there an overwhelming presence of one race? Are the positions of power in fashion disproportionately filled by a given race of people? Whiteness and white people are exponentially more present and in places of power in the fashion industry.

Racism is also about the DECISIONS and DEFINITIONS that result when and where power is present. When a given race of people is more present in positions of power, then they get to make most of the decisions. Furthermore, the decisions that are made often define, in this case, what "is" fashionable and beautiful. Essence magazine was created in part to resist the injurious results of black women's lack of presence and power to make decisions and create definitions in the world in which they live. This includes the fashion world. So, when Michaela Davis says that Essence has a responsibility to live up to their name, brand, and motto of prioritizing black women by hiring black women, she is attempting to fight against the reality and results of a preexisting and present racism that exists through the overwhelming presence, power, decision-making, and definition-creating whiteness in the fashion industry. This is not reverse racism, it is anti-racism. It is an attempt to fight the racism in the fashion industry to have a place where black women can be present and powerful. It is an effort to fight racism to create a space where black women can decide and define what is fashionable.

Yet, what does all this have to do with Jesus? Let me ease your mind and tell you that I do not think that Jesus has a real stake in fashion. I don't believe Jesus prefers paisley over polka dot, stripes over plaids, Rocawear over Sean John, or Michael Kors over Louis Vuitton. I do believe that the ministry of Jesus is concerned for the last and gives priority to those who society has cast off as the least. In terms of gender, this would be women. In terms of economics, this would be the poor. In terms of sexuality, this would be the LGBTQI community. In terms of health, this would be the diseased and differently abled. And in terms of race, this would be people of color in America. Does Jesus care about race in a preferential sense? NO!!! But does Jesus care about those who may be mistreated and misused because of their race (... Even when this marginalization is found in the fashion industry)? ABSOLUTELY!!! So, just because Jesus does not ultimately care about race, Jesus does absolutely care about racism .... And so should those who call themselves his followers.

Questions

1. Do you see any racial bias in the fashion industry?

2. What responsibility do followers of Jesus have in the realm of racial justice?

45

Pet Store Religion

While studying at Starbucks the other day, a lady and her young, energetic, cute, and cuddly puppy caught my eye. It was a young Golden Retriever that had all the vibrancy of an animal that had seen nothing but the best days and simply yearned for fun, frolicking, and Love. I began to reminisce about the best moments of my former life as a dog owner – the unfailing enthusiasm that Cosmo and Manhattan (my two yorkies) would have each and every time I walked in the door; the moments cuddled on the couch watching TV; the time I had to save them from drowning in a duck pond on a golf course after they chased ducks and realized they weren't the best swimmers when they got in the deepest waters. Then I began thinking about the money spent on toys, food, and trips to the veterinarian, the many mornings I had to walk them and did not feel like getting up, the times I had to provide for their care in my absence on a trip or vacation, or the hours spent cleaning carpet from potty training and slip ups. I soon realized why many people Love going to the pet store or playing with other people's dogs, but somehow never take the next step to buy a dog. Most of us want the cute-ness and the cuddly-ness of playing with a puppy without the commitment of possessing and being responsible for a life. I call this a pet store mentality.

Even when I reflect on the complaints of many of my sisters in Christ and humanity, I realize that many women charge men with some version of this phenomenon. It is often said that men want the privileges of companionship, without the responsibilities of commitment. Can you imagine that!?!? Somehow, and for some reason, some women have in their minds that a man will want to take a woman out, bring a woman in, and get advice, attention, and affection from her, all the while not wanting to be supportive of her dreams, responsible for her feelings, or faithful to their relationship. I know, I know. Many of you are asking where I get some of these crazy ideas. Nevertheless, many of us (men and women) have a pet store mentality when it comes to relationships. We are always ready for the fun and festivities of having company, but hesitant to give the dedication, discipline, and sacrifice of making a commitment. I call this a pet store relationship.

Unfortunately, the pet store mentality creeps into many of our spiritual lives. Many of us want to enjoy the benefits of worship and the blessings of God in our lives, without ever deeply considering God's call on our lives and what God would have us do with our lives. So we go to church on Sunday hoping to receive the joy of community, the inspiration of good music, or the encouragement of "a Word," all the while never quite ready to cut out some of our social time in order to serve, lend our talents and gifts for ministry, or sacrifice any of our money for higher purposes. Just like that cute little puppy Golden Retriever at Starbucks needs more than a pat on the forehead, a scratch behind the ear, or a rub on the belly, God (and YOUR SPIRIT for that matter) needs more than attendance on Sunday, a holy e-mail forward, or a facebook shout-out. Nevertheless most of us are content to want God to move, without ever moving us; happy asking God to work in our lives, without wanting God to use our lives for God's work. I call this pet store religion.

Questions

1. Where in your life have you been guilty of a "pet store" mentality?

2. What are some of the costs of care for your spirit and a relationship with God?

46
Preachers or Puppets?

One of the things that saddens me about the political landscape of our times are the positions or lack thereof of some of our clergy. Though I don't believe that it should be an ethical imperative that clergy, or particularly Black clergy, be on the political "left" on every issue, I do believe that there are preachers across the landscape of America that continue to show they are short sighted, simple-minded, and/or spineless.

One of the saddest Christian trends of our political culture is the provincial thinking that attempts to make Christianity exclusively about our stances on abortion and same gender Love. I have a problem with clergy who are ready to send people to hell about the "right to life," but won't speak against innocent people dying as a result of American military strikes, unarmed people dying as a result of police violence, or sick children dying due to inaccessible health care. Yes, unborn children have a right to live, but so do poor children in our own country, and innocent war victims outside our country. Not only are many of these right-wing reverends inconsistent about life, but they are also extremely selective on when it is time to listen to Jesus and when it is not. Whether we like it or not, Jesus was pro poor, anti-capitalist, and a champion of his followers going above and beyond for the least, the lost, and the left behind. I am amazed how Christian people and pastors acrobatically champion the Christian Love ethic inside the walls of their church, but act as if it is irrelevant to their politics. If any Christian is serious about Jesus, we have to ask ourselves some far reaching questions. Where would a Jesus who believed in the last being first and giving good news to the poor stand on universal healthcare? Would God care about our toxic violence to the earth that God created and asked us to be good stewards? What about economic policies that cater to the haves and is not authentically concerned with the have nots? The point here is that making Christianity a two-issue religion when it comes to politics is extremely small minded and does not take the life and ministry of Jesus seriously. We should be offended when Christians minimize the profundity of Christianity to become intellectual puppets of political characters for the sake of a two-issue platform.

To understand another form of puppetry with our preachers, we have to go all the way back to 2000. George Bush was initially elected in part by his ability to garner the support of Christian pastors all across America. By using some of the rhetoric that I have just talked about and by offering the now famous "Faith-Based Initiatives", many "Dr.'s", Bishops, and Apostles encouraged their congregations to vote for Bush. Black preachers who had never supported a republican agenda found themselves pushing a Bush presidency with the hopes of gaining federal dollars. At the sound of money and the hopes of feeling like they had more political clout, our Pastors clamored after Bush and suggested we should too. This was all done in the name of the Lord and the promotion of Christian issues. Yet when the same Bush did not deliver on the goods, and the "Faith-Based Initiatives" that were promised went overwhelmingly under-funded and ignored by the Bush administration, the same preachers would not and did not publicly criticize Bush. Fast forward eighteen years and now preachers who were too loud over the false promises of Bush are now too quiet during the ethical perversity of Trump. The idea that preachers on the right won't loudly condemn the justice seeking policies the Trump administration continue to attack, the racism Trump continues to exhibit, the sexist and misogynistic way Trump continues to devalue and demean women, and the profound public pettiness Trump continues to espouse is mind boggling to me. Trump uses fear and xenophobia to reduce immigrants and immigration policy to MS-13 gang members, and right winged, but not right-minded preachers, remain silent.

Is Christianity stuck with pastors who will take a hard line about the sanctity of embryos and fetuses but won't speak up about the dignity of born and living humans domestically and from "shithole" countries? Are we stuck with Christians who will bash the Love of same gender relationships but won't whisper about the hate, sexual violence, racism, and derisive rhetoric that comes from the White House? Are we stuck with preachers who will jump through hoops about women being sexually pure but won't lift a finger to help women be sexually safe from predators? If clergy does not get the moral courage to follow the radical teaching of Jesus Christ when it is politically convenient or not, we will be stuck with pulpit puppets in a time that desperately needs public prophets. We need complex thinking and authentic conviction from our preachers. This does not mean they will be democrats or will always vote with the left. However, the last thing we need from preachers is them giving us a simplified political gospel or living by an "if it doesn't make dollars it doesn't make sense" creed. We don't need puppets who are slave to any party or president. We need preachers who are radical followers of that plebeian people Lover from a ghetto called Nazareth.

Questions

1. How do you connect the Love ethic of Jesus and his concern for the poor with your politics?

2. How do you determine which political issues (if any) should be influenced by your faith?

47

Preparing to Fast

Each year, often in February the Christian season of Lent begins. The forty days leading to Easter comprise the season of Lent. Many of us participate or create some type of fast in which we take these forty days to give up something we would normally not go without. Yet, as many of us enter this season plotting and planning what we will go without, I want to raise a white flag of warning so that we may not miss the profound possibilities that this season has to offer.

On the one hand, fasting during Lent has become so commonplace, and even popular amongst some, that it runs the risk of becoming perfunctory. Whenever we begin to take part in an exercise week after week, month after month, and year after year, it can become so familiar to us that it loses its ability to touch us in a new way or impact us in a profound way. The second risk we run when we fast is making our fast about us. No, I don't mean the bragging and boasting that we do to friends and family about what we are giving up and the tremendous toll that it is taking on our lives (though that has its problems). However, we often make fasting a competition with ourselves to see if we can make it forty days without this or that. As a result, we either become disappointed in ourselves if we fail to make it, or we assume a posture of pride about the accomplishment of making forty days of fasting.

Whether we allow our fasting to become perfunctory or ourselves to become prideful, both of these distract us from the true purpose of this spiritual practice. In the end, fasting is about God and our relationship with God. It is

136

the abstaining from one thing to focus on an-Other. It is the withdrawal from one thing so that we can withdraw into an-Other. It is not to see how we can test or challenge ourselves, but rather how we can shorten the bridge between ourselves and God. Also, as a spiritual practice, it gives us an opportunity to practice saying no to something we would ordinarily like or do. At the same time, it gives us an opportunity to practice saying yes to spiritual virtues like sacrifice, renunciation, simplicity, and prayer.

I pray that the next time you fast or enter the season of Lent, you commit yourself to connecting your spirit with the Spirit of God. As you enter into the season that celebrates the resurrection power of God, I pray that you meditate and concentrate on what it is in you that God can bring back to life. I pray that this season of Lent will find new meaning and power in your spiritual life and that you become better and closer to God in the process.

Questions

1. How would you describe the power of fasting?

2. What could you, or even should you, fast from that would bring you closer to God?

48

Cleaning Up a Mess

The other day I was at one of my favorite mobile offices in Midtown, Atlanta – Starbucks. It seems at least once a month I have begun a tradition of purchasing a Grande Hot Tea (usually Jade Citrus Mint), and then spilling the whole thing while I try to add my honey and turbinado sugar (I feel extremely bourgeois telling this story). So there went my tea all over my table and all over the floor, and out of embarrassment I quickly grabbed a handful of napkins and tried to start cleaning this spill up. Napkin by napkin became lost in a sea of hot tea, and I was overwhelmed with a mess that I made but was having the hardest time cleaning up.

Finally, a barista saw my mess, saw me frantically failing at cleaning it up, and said, "Sir, you don't have to do that, I'll get it." A few seconds later she came with a towel and a mop. A few swipes of the towel and a few pushes of the mop, and what I had struggled to do with my tools, she easily did with hers. I am sure had I made a slight spill, she would have allowed me to use a napkin or two to wipe it up. But the spill was too large, had gone into too many areas, and was taking up too many napkins for her to sit idly by and watch me continue striving to fix what I had messed up. All I needed was clumsiness to make the mess, but I needed tools that I didn't have to clean that same mess up. It suddenly dawned on me that while I was well equipped to make a mess, I was ill equipped to clean it up. Do I need to tell you that at this point my sermonic antennae went up?

My Starbuck's experience mirrors so many moments of my life, and my barista's reaction mirrors so many responses of my God. So often I find myself caught in the reality that it takes infinitely less effort to make a mess than to clean it up. Often I feel like the napkins I am using are being drowned by the mess. My efforts are inefficient, my strivings are insufficient and my tools are inadequate. In these moments I feel overwhelmed and often I make the desperate decision to give up. Sometimes I feel doomed to have and live in messes that are beyond my capacity to clean. Throughout my life I have single handedly made messes that spill over into other areas of my life, affect other people in my life, and become so huge that I am powerless to clean them up.

This seems to be a law of life. Often we find ourselves well equipped to make messes, but ill equipped to clean them up. It seems much easier to break than to fix, to tear down than to build up, to destroy than to make whole. Just consider something as simple as a reputation or a relationship. It can take years to build either, and one or two terrible decisions to destroy both. Yet, Starbucks' baristas are not the only people who clean up messes that they do not make. There are times when God sees our mess, observes our futile attempts to clean it up, and steps in with bigger and better tools to heal what we've hurt, fix what we've broken, and wipe away what we've spilled. I walked away from that Starbucks, not only grateful that there was someone there to help me with my mess, but determined to be honest the next time I was in such a situation and ask for help. That barista was there to not only serve me if I needed tea, but help me if I made a mess. Likewise, we have a God that is willing and waiting to utilize God's divine power to make up the difference where we fall short. Though I think we all have a responsibility to grab napkins and do what we can to address our mistakes, I am glad that GRACE exists to make up the difference where we fall short. Yes, mercy suits our case and that classic hymn still applies to our lives - "Amazing Grace, how sweet the sound that saved a wretch like me ..."

Think Deeper

Questions

1. What was the last mess you made by yourself but needed help cleaning up?

2. What do you need God to help you clean up right now?

49

Putting the Pieces Together

I now understand why many advise against the coaching and teaching of your own child. Having worked with children and youth for years, I have developed a substantial amount of patience while teaching. That slowly built patience quickly goes out of the window with my own child. I am not sure if it is because of the personal relationship or my desire for the best in my child raises my expectations and exigency; but, when I am teaching Bryce, I find myself trying to hold back anger, lowering my voice, or taking deep breaths constantly. Now, if at this moment you are scoffing at me and reading in shame, then I am going to ask that you stop and pray for me. I am a parent in progress.

One of my teaching frustrations with Bryce would always occur when we did puzzles together. To his credit, Bryce started doing puzzles when he was two years old and he learned to do them relatively well. However, one of the things that took me years to get Bryce to understand is that you can look at the picture on the box, and it can help you to put your pieces together. As a two and three-year old, my child was obsessed with simply picking up two pieces and twisting and turning them until they fit, or he just lost hope and picked up another piece and started all over again. I would constantly beg Bryce to look at the box because it will tell you where the pieces go. The box gives you a picture of what these scattered pieces can look like. More importantly, looking at the box can save you so much time and frustration from trying to make sense of it all without guidance. My constant plea to Bryce was simply to remind him that, "The box can help you."

Beloved, I believe Bryce's early problem with puzzles reflects many of our present problems in our lives. In many ways, our life is like an undone puzzle. There are pieces everywhere that when scattered don't make any sense and cause confusion and discord. These pieces include our gifts and talents, strengths and weaknesses, joys and pains, past experiences and future aspirations. Many of our biggest struggles come when we try to figure out our lives one piece at a time. Like Bryce, we may get it at some point and every now and then we happen to get lucky and pick up the right pieces at the right time and they fit beautifully together. Yet, we are also living in unnecessary confusion, needless frustration, and making avoidable mistakes because we are refusing to look at the picture God has given us in the life and ministry of Jesus Christ. God has created us and given us all the pieces we need to make a beautiful picture out of our lives. In the midst of our current confusion and present irritation are the components of a healthy and whole life. We have everything we need to be beautiful. All of our experiences, expertise, character traits, and virtues can combine to make a complete and clear picture. All we have to do now is look at the picture on the box. Jesus' life of revolutionary Love, intentional spirituality, and perpetual purpose serves as a model for all of us who are trying to put our pieces together. Our best and most beautiful self is waiting for us to get it together. You don't have to put pieces together alone. "The box can help you."

Questions

1. What part(s) of your life are not coming together right now?

2. How would your life look differently if you used the life and ministry of Jesus as your model

I am still learning to Love. The better I Love the better my life. However, I cannot Love better without thinking deeper about Love (see what I just did there?). For most of my adult life I have been wrestling with, thinking about, and trying to live in Love. In my thirties, I came to the crushing realization that I did not Love well. I am still not sure I Love well now. Yet, I am convinced that a part of my problem with Loving well was my belief that Love had more to do with feelings than actions. When I thought about Love, I mostly thought about how it made me feel. I longed to feel Loved, and I cherished feeling deeply about others. Yet, somehow for me what I actually did seemed less important than how I felt. Many of us are this way with Love, and with God. We see our relationship with God as one that should be defined by how deeply we feel about God, not how we live in the world, but feelings don't do the work of Love.

Instinctually, Love begins with feelings; however, it is consummated and completed with actions. There is no one we Love well without acting for the purpose of their improvement, welfare, or delight. Likewise, we don't Love God well without a lived commitment to God's purposes and plans. How we live and what we do has everything to do with how we Love. Unless how we feel moves and motivates us to action, our feelings have little to do with Love. Since Love is ultimately an action, Love has personal, relational, social, and political consequences.

Love without action is sentimental. Sentimental Love ultimately destroys us. It asks too little and accepts too much. It risks nothing, costs nothing, and delivers little. Sentimental Love asks victims to forgive without asking perpetrators to repent. Sentimental Love asks for feelings without actions and words without deeds. Sentimental Love celebrates the actions of God's Love for us, without moving us to act for God. Sentimental Love asks women who have been victims of sexism to forgive without asking men who are sexist to change. Sentimental Love asks for racial reconciliation without racial reparations. For too long our understanding of Love has been sappy and sentimental. In some ways, I hope this section moves us to deepen our engagement with the idea of Love. I pray it pushes us to Love ourselves more dearly, challenges us to Love others more actively, and moves us to consider Love beyond how it manifests itself personally.

The one thing that has kept me Christian throughout my deepest doubts and fiercest moments of skepticism, is that I believe in Love. When Jesus is asked, what is the greatest commandment, he responds by saying that Loving God, Loving our neighbor, and Loving ourselves (the Loving ourselves is implied) is the best we can do. He then says something equally important when he says all the prophets and laws hang on this law of Love. Jesus says that all the preached and written words of their religion were working up to them learning how to Love better. Ultimately, learning to Love better is our greatest human achievement and it is the point of our spirituality.
Love is hard. I hope the next few pages help us to "do" it better.

50
I Believe in Love

I am constantly and consistently reminded of the power of Love. Some years ago I began the arduous but gratifying task of reading the signature biographical tome on Warren Buffet's life – The Snowball. In the twentieth chapter the author, Alice Schroeder, explains the important role Buffet's wife Susie had in making him feel Lovable. After growing up with a loyal but emotionally abusive mother, Schroeder concludes that Leila (Buffet's mother) "had convinced both Warren and Doris (Buffet's sister) that deep down they were worthless." I was moved as Schroeder quoted Buffett's explanation on what Susie meant to him.

Buffet explains,
I had all these defense mechanisms that she could explain, but I can't. She probably saw things in me that other people couldn't see. But she knew it would take time and a lot of nourishment to bring it out. She made me feel that I had somebody with a little sprinkling can who was going to make sure that the flowers grew .... I needed her like crazy. I was happy in my work, but I wasn't happy with myself. She literally saved my life She resurrected me. She put me together. It was the same kind of unconditional love you would get from a parent.

What Buffet explains is exactly what Love does to us and for us and why we need Love in our lives. Love finds the best and the strongest in us when the common eye can only see the worst and the weakest. It waters and warms us so that we can bloom and bud at our best and brightest. It literally saves us from the death of loneliness and isolation.

IN THE WORST TIMES, LOVE LIFTS US. IN THE HARDEST TIMES, LOVE SOOTHES US. IN THE COLDEST TIMES, LOVE WARMS US.

All at once it is our biggest romantic engine, our best political tool, our strongest familial ally, and the greatest and most ubiquitous force in our world.

The Bible says, "God IS Love (1 John 4:8)." I think we often miss the profundity of this claim. So many times we look for God by hoping for miracles, begging for money, or searching for materialistic gain. All the while, God's presence in our lives and God's power through our lives exists in the Loving relationships that we live in day to day. God IS Love. This means that God literally is the connection we feel with our friends, the nourishment we receive from our parents, the enthusiastic longing we have for our "boo," the loyalty we have for our boys or our girlfriends, and the undying bond we have with extended family. To say I believe in Love IS to say I believe in God. This is why I can find no better subject to talk about, no better idea to think about, or no better force to embrace. Love … I believe in it!!! Though I believe in it deeply, this does not mean I excel at it greatly. Nevertheless, I believe the greatest endeavor each of us has in this world is to live in it … to live in Love.

51
These Three Words

What if I told you there are three words that are more difficult to say than "I Love you," and at times are more important?

Years ago, when my favorite player was nearing the end of his four-year tenure playing with the Miami Heat, I saw something that I have never seen in my sports watching career. If you know me then you know that player is none other than Lebron James, and whatever team he plays on becomes my defacto favorite team. Yet, one night Lebron James' stock went up volumes in my book.

The Heat were pretty much being dominated by their conference rivals the Indiana Pacers and were making terrible mistakes to top it off. During a timeout Lebron James got so infuriated with what his teammate, Mario Chalmers, was saying to him that he jumped up in his face and both had to be grabbed so a fight would not commence. Now if anyone has played or watched sports they know there is nothing new about teammates losing their cool and almost coming to blows in the "heat of battle." However what happened later blew my mind.

Later, in the same game, a camera caught a second conversation, that at least on camera was a monologue initiated by Lebron James. He looked at the same teammate he jumped up to fight earlier and said these words, "Rio, Rio (the nickname for Mario), I was wrong, my bad." While pounding on his chest to non-verbally accent his words, Lebron James, the best player on his team and in the world, one of the highest paid athletes in the world, the most decorated player of this decade, the most recognizable athlete on the planet, owned his fault and said, "I was wrong." If that were not enough, because Lebron James knew he had been publicly seen squabbling with his teammate, he promptly made a public apology by tweeting the following after the game: *"I love @mchalmers15 like a blood brother! I was wrong and apologized to him!"* Maybe this is not the first time someone who has all the ingredients to have an oversized ego has initiated an apology both privately and publicly and completely acknowledged fault with no ifs, ands, or buts. It is the first time I have ever seen such a thing being done without it being initiated by public scrutiny or media pressure. I still have seen no one take this much responsibility and go out of their way to publicly apologize with no caveats or qualifications. Whether it is the first or only time is not the point. The significance is still the same.

We often hear about the importance of "these three words" called 'I Love you.' So much is made about how difficult it is and how important it is to say I Love you. However, I submit, "I was wrong," may be three equally important and even more difficult words to express. In fact, think about it, which three words have you said more often and more recently?

FOR MOST OF US, IT IS EASIER TO EXPRESS LOVE THAN TO OWN FAULT.

However, so many of our romantic relationships would be better, family ties would be closer, and friendships would be healthier if we could learn how to accept and own, out loud, that there are times where we are wrong. I am sure that as you read this right now you can think of someone who you owe an, "I was wrong," but your pride, anger, or frustration has not brought you to say it.

Our spiritual health is dependent on high self-esteem, but just as importantly, our spirituality begs us to be self-critical enough and honest enough to become aware AND acknowledge when we are wrong. This week, or maybe even this day, I challenge you to muster up the courage to not only know when you are wrong, but to look someone in the eye, touch yourself on the chest, and say out loud these three words: "I WAS WRONG."

52

An Unknown Masterpiece

In the fall of 2013, a recent discovery rocked the art world. An original painting of Vincent van Gogh was discovered after being discarded and dismissed as a fake for over one hundred years. The "Sunset at Montmajour," estimated to now be worth tens of millions of dollars, was stored away for decades in the obscurity of someone's attic. It was in the collection of Vincent's brother until his widow sold it to an art dealer in Paris who later sold it to a Norwegian dealer. Soon after, it was "declared" a fake, and began its one-hundred-year journey of being unknown, unwanted, and undervalued.

Meditate on that! An artistic masterpiece was tucked away, unknown to the public, and dismissed by art historians because no one knew its real creator. What a tragedy! All because outside observers got it wrong, this wonderful work of art was hidden, tossed aside, and rejected. Yet, today the same piece that was hidden and neglected is now displayed and spotlighted. The same piece that was irrelevant for decades, is now invaluable. People have flocked to see it, media has rushed to cover it, and collectors may be lining up to buy it. It has gone from worthless to priceless all because we now know who created it.

I began to wonder how many of us have lived a "Sunset at Montmajour" existence. How many of us have allowed outside observers to underestimate, under-appreciate and undervalue us? More importantly, how many of us have begun to believe about ourselves what others have "declared" about us? How many times as a result of being rejected, neglected, and/or dismissed have we begun to tuck away our talents, make ourselves small, and hide our best selves? How many of us are hidden when we should be displayed, marginalized when we should be cherished, or neglected when we should be spotlighted?

The thing about the "Sunset of Montmajour" is that not one thing about it has changed since it was created, except outside opinion.

IT WAS ALWAYS REAL, EVEN WHEN NO ONE KNEW IT. IT WAS ALWAYS VALUABLE, EVEN IF NO ONE THOUGHT IT. IT WAS ALWAYS GREAT, EVEN IF NO ONE ACKNOWLEDGED IT. SUCH IS THE CASE WITH YOU!

You are valuable, your worth is immeasurable, and your gifts are made to be shared with the world. The thing that makes a Van Gogh painting priceless is the same thing that makes you precious and prized – your Creator. The difference in you and the "Sunset at Montmajour" is that you don't have to wait for someone else to connect your life to your Creator. You are created, preserved, and sustained by God. This means you don't have to be bound by outside opinion, and you cannot afford to be convinced that you are not a masterpiece. Once the world believed the painting was from the great Van Gogh, it changed the very nature of how the world treated that work of art. Once you believe the greatness of your origins, you can live into becoming the tour de force you were created to be. You are God's artwork .... LIVE LIKE IT!

53
Other's Tastes Don't Determine Your Flavor

For whatever reason, it both tickles and momentarily disappoints me when my child does not have my tastes. For some reason I think he should Love any and everything that I Love, especially when it comes to sweets. I realized one day when Bryce was much younger that I had never introduced him to a McDonald's apple pie. As I always do, I began picturing how Bryce's world would be turned upside down when I introduced him to yet another delight that his inexperienced taste buds had never savored. I began reminiscing about the old "fried" apple pies from McDonalds. You know the old rectangular desserts that had these huge bubbles on them, and used to come in a piece of paper. Well, the paper has turned into a box and the fried has become baked, but I still Love a McDonald's apple pie every now and then. Don't judge me!

So we had come to the end of our meal, the moment of my glory had arrived, and I pulled the apple pie out. Both asking and telling I said, "You have never had an apple pie from McDonald's, have you?" Bryce acknowledged that he had not, but he did not have the excitement and enthusiasm that I expected. So, I handed him the apple pie, he took a bite, and began to chew reflectively.

> Too anxious to wait, I asked, "So, do you like it?"
> Bryce calmly handed me the apple pie back and even more matter-of-factly said, "No, I don't like it."

I popped it in my mouth to make sure Bryce had not received some alternative recipe or mis-seasoned apple pie. As I chewed and swallowed, I was certain this was the apple pie that I had known and Loved, but my son had no chemistry with, attraction to, or appreciation for my beloved apple pie. Now as one who has had the apple pie, I know there is nothing wrong with the apple pie. It is warm, seasoned well, and tasty. As a Lover of the apple pie, I am not less convinced about its merits, and I do not blame the apple pie for Bryce not liking it. I simply have to accept that Bryce has the right and in fact does not like a perfectly made Mc Donald's apple pie.

Now stay with me!!! At this point I begin to imagine me being the apple pie, or the apple pie being me. If the apple pie was me, it would start doubting itself because Bryce did not like it. It would begin to wonder if it was warm enough, seasoned enough, or tasty enough to deserve to be liked. It would begin to think it did not have enough cinnamon, enough apples, or enough crust to please my child. When the truth is, it is perfectly made and no less good just because Bryce does not care for it. Bryce's "tastes" do not determine the worth, value, or flavor of the pie. In fact Bryce's tastes are really all about him and not about the quality of the pie.

Many of us often struggle to Love ourselves because we allow other people's tastes to determine how we feel about our flavor. If we were to be honest we would admit that we have struggled with self-esteem, wrestled with self-image, and felt less of ourselves because someone did not like us, was not attracted to us, or just did not have a taste for us. However, Bryce and that apple pie taught me something that day.

WE CAN BE PERFECTLY MADE AND STILL NOT BE LIKED BY SOMEONE. WE CAN BE SEASONED JUST RIGHT AND STILL NOT BE PLEASING TO ANOTHER PERSON'S TASTE

This is not a statement about our flavor; this is a statement about that person's tastes. We are "fearfully and wonderfully made." That does not mean that everybody likes us. However, God has made us with just the right warmth, just the right seasoning, and from the right recipe. So walk tall, stand proud, and live in whoever God has made you because other's tastes don't determine your flavor.

54

Dear Young Black Women

In 2012 Pastor Creflo Dollar was accused of abusing his then 15-year old daughter. Being a world-renowned preacher and megachurch pastor, this quickly became national news and a hot topic on social media. I know just as little now as I did then about his guilt or innocence. Pastor Dollar's guilt or innocence is not mine to know. I do know I was profoundly disappointed at the responses to a teenage girl who was allegedly choked, slapped, and hit with a shoe. So many people who knew just as little as I did resorted to an instinct to defend the man and attack the girl. I am often hurt when we attack potential victims without evidence. Who we are naturally inclined to defend when we don't know the facts tells so much about how and who we are taught to Love and hate. Unfortunately time after time in our society, our instinct tells us to be suspicious of women and children. Particularly black women and children. This public and common suspicion led me to write the following letter to young black women.

Dear Young Black Women,

I am writing you with a profoundly heavy heart to say I am sorry. What brings me to this apology is the response to the latest incident between one of you and yet another prominent black man. Again we are forced to ask the question, "Did a black man abuse a young black woman?" Again we are forced to face the possibility of abuse. And again I am saddened about what seems to be a pattern of people in our community making Loving you, protecting you, and fighting for you the least of our priorities. It hurts that when faced with the possibility of your abuse we can find any reason to blame you and defend your possible attackers. When a grown man, allegedly R. Kelly, had sex, videoed, and urinated on one of your thirteen-year olds, so many thought it was important to point out that she looked like she knew what she was doing and that clearly it was not her first time. So many people thought the most important question to ask was, "Why was she even there?" "When did she start having sex?" "Where did she learn to do those acts?" A grown man urinates on a girl, and we want to start the conversation by interrogating the girl and/or her mother. When Rihanna got out of that car battered and bruised, so many of us began the conversation with a question. "What did she say or do to provoke that kind of behavior?" Others wanted to assume she must have hit him first. While yet others wanted to lecture women about the importance of not provoking men to physical wrath. We did not know what happened in the limo, but we do know what came out of it—a virtually scratch-less man and a beaten woman. Yet, numerous people thought we needed to begin by interrogating the actions of the woman.

Now here we are again with the recent allegations of Creflo Dollar—a father allegedly slapping, choking, throwing down, and hitting a girl with a shoe. We don't know what happened and should not pretend to know. However, we don't have to know what happened in this particular incident to articulate where we stand on the very possibility of abuse to young girls. We don't have to know the details of this episode, or whether he is guilty or innocent, to unequivocally declare there is a line that should not be crossed when it comes to the safety and well-being of our black girls. What we do know is how many have responded to the prospect of another young girl being abused. Many seem to argue that if she was disrespectful, then whatever happened was justified. Others want to begin the conversation with a diagnosis of this era of children as the most disrespectful in history. Then there are those who dedicate a sentence to expressing how they don't condone abuse, followed by a paragraph explaining why violence may sometimes be called for with disrespectful children. Scores of people are most concerned with what the girl said or what she did to be disrespectful. Again we are faced with the possibility of abuse, and again we are faced with the interrogation of the person who was potentially abused. What hurts me so profoundly is the pattern our community has developed of not standing up for black girls; the custom we have made of not making abuse the priority deserving our most immediate attention.

THERE IS A HABIT, AN INSTINCT IT SEEMS, OF WANTING TO PUT ABUSED, OR EVEN POSSIBLY ABUSED, BLACK GIRLS ON THE WITNESS STAND TO CROSS EXAMINE THEM AND THEN SHOW THEM HOW THEIR ABUSE IS THEIR OWN FAULT.

Whether it is a teenager who is too "fast," a girlfriend who is too "sassy," or a teenage girl who is too "disrespectful," the message is clear to our black girls. You are your own problem.

Why are we prone to leave black girls unprotected and undefended? Where did we learn to not take black girls' lives seriously? When will we make Loving, safe, and equal treatment of black girls a priority of the highest order? I don't know the answers to these questions, but until something changes I will remain sorry. Sorry that Christians, first and foremost, do not always find a way to connect the gospel of Christ to the need to prioritize black girls and their abuse, even when it is alleged. Sorry that our instincts are to dismiss, disbelieve, or disregard your abuse. Sorry that again and again we leave you to fend for yourselves.

Humbly in Christ's Love,

B.A. Jackson

55
A Letter to Chris Brown

Dear Chris Brown,

I know you will probably never get this letter, but my need to write it far exceeds my need for you to receive it. I am not writing as a stellar paradigm of Love nor as a supreme example of how a man should treat a woman. I am writing because I too, like most everyone, am deeply flawed. Still, I believe in our worst moments we need community and not exile. You are facing a period in your life where the possibility of your vices overshadowing your virtues, at least in the public's eye, seems more real than ever. However, you are not alone! All of us struggle with the tension between the best in us and the worst in us. The truth is we are all afraid that someday the path the best in us can deliver will be detoured by what the worst in us can destroy. So I write not to look down on you, but simply just to share brother to brother.

I am writing because I am afraid. I am fearful that you might buy in even more to the sexism and misogyny that plagues and permeates our world. Patriarchy has a way of always turning the critical questions on the woman whenever there is a problem in a heterosexual romantic relationship. This is why there have been both men and women who seemed to be more concerned about what Rihanna did instead of what had been done to her. Though I know it is almost impossible to completely cleanse the stain of sexism out of our thinking and acting, I do hope that you will at least peek behind the curtain of patriarchy long enough to see the problem with rationalizing why or how a woman can "provoke" a man to hitting or beating her.

I am afraid that without a self-critical look at yourself, you will hit a woman again … and again. The patriarchy of our world teaches us that being in control is a part of what it means to be a man. Yet, so often in our relationships with women we find we are not in control. In precarious moments like these we are physical to assert whatever control we can. However, when the last control we can hold onto is physical control, then we've lost control! Yet, here is where the problem lies: the very idea that we should "control" our women is based on them being objects and not human. We cannot and should not control anyone but ourselves. In the end, we have to hope our call on another's life can influence them enough to treat us the way we long to be treated. If not, we have to control ourselves enough, amidst the hurt of this realization, to let it go.

I am also writing because I am hurt. I am hurt by all the people who have given up on you. To be sure, I too believe that Rihanna made the wrong move by coming back to you and the relationship so soon. If she was not going to break it off forever, she should have, at a minimum, waited until you had proven over time your commitment to working on and changing your behavior. Nevertheless, it pains me to hear Oprah Winfrey, a sister I dearly admire, and others, adamantly declare: "He will hit you again." I understand where they are coming from, and I know the probability of recurrence shown by statistics. Yet, as a Christian I believe in one idea that those who deny your ameliorative capacities are not appealing to – conversion.

I BELIEVE IN A GOD WHO LOVES US AT OUR WORST AND CHALLENGES US TO LOVE EACH OTHER THE SAME WAY.

I know what it feels like for someone to give up on you. So I am writing to tell you in Love, that though I think you were inexcusably wrong, I am praying for your conversion. Not the conversion that is reduced to platitudes of what Jesus did on a hill far away, but rather a mental, spiritual, and physical redirection of our life and understanding. Without conversion, you won't have the power to overcome the forces of abuse, patriarchy, and misogyny that influence domestic violence. Without conversion, when you feel deeply hurt or helplessly out of control, you will hit again. But I have to believe that the last time you were violent can be the last time you will ever be violent. So, may God's Love be with you, and may you forever take the challenge to live in Love.

Always in Love,

B.A. Jackson

56

Snow Warms the Heart

On January 28, 2014 the Atlanta metropolitan area was crippled by one of the biggest snow storms in recent history. At noon that day all was well, but by 2:00pm disaster had hit Atlanta like I have never seen before in over 20 years. A snow storm bringing about 2 inches of snow covered the ground and iced the roads; seemingly the entire highway system in Atlanta became a parking lot. People abandoned cars, walked miles, or just remained stuck hopelessly awaiting relief. Children were stuck in cars, school buses, and schools. Panic began to strike families, friends and loved ones everywhere. Again we were shown how vulnerable, powerless, and precarious we are to the whims of Mother Nature.

I was also amazed by how these moments of extreme emergency brought out the best of our humanity, compassion, and generosity. There was story after story of people walking up and down the highways to make sure children had food, liquids, and warm coverings. I ran into a man who had walked over four miles through the course of the night, when finally he was given the refuge of shelter by a complete stranger. Adults in neighborhoods in close proximity to schools where children were stuck brought food, blankets, and sleeping bags. In the midst of being frozen and iced by snow, hearts were being warmed and people were being moved to spring into doing what they could to ameliorate and alleviate the damage of this disaster.

Imagine that! For a brief moment, many chose to prioritize attending to the needs of people right where they were, instead of concerning themselves with how exactly they got there. I am sure there were people who could have made better decisions, parents who could have been more aggressive and proactive about ensuring the safety of their child, and officials who could have planned and prepared in a more excellent manner. Yet, in the midst of the exigency of this frozen calamity, so many people chose to suspend asking who was responsible and who was to blame, and chose to allow the needs of the victimized and vulnerable call them into action.

It took the disaster of ice-covered roads, traffic jammed highways, abandoned cars, and displaced men, women, and children to move us to the action I believe God calls us to embody every single day.

EACH DAY I BELIEVE WE HAVE OPPORTUNITIES TO SEE AND MEET THE NEEDS OF THE MOST VULNERABLE AND VICTIMIZED OF OUR SOCIETY.

During every election and voting opportunity we are given the chance to make policies that will save children who are stuck, unattended, under cared for, and unLoved. There are times when problems are so severe, needs are so salient, and crises are so pronounced that all else should take second priority to lending a hand, sacrificing ourselves, and taking action. Some believe these situations are once in a blue moon. I believe these opportunities call us every day. The occasional heroism shown in Atlanta's snowstorm is simply a reminder of the everyday call God gives us to Love.

57

Eat Your Vegetables

Parenting has changed me! Some of the things I was against as a child, I now advocate as a parent. One such thing is eating vegetables. Like many children, when I was a child, I usually found eating vegetables detestable. It took pushing, prodding, bribing, and sometimes spanking to get me to finish the green, nasty stuff on my plate. However, as a parent, I find myself blessed to be burdened with the responsibility of taking care of my child. Instinctually, I want the very best for my son, and taking care of him means working towards his intellectual, spiritual, and physical flourishing. And, yes, this has meant me becoming an advocate for vegetables. Now I must be honest, I may not be blazing any advocacy trails when it comes to vegetables, but I have done my share of insisting, demanding, and yes bribing so that Bryce will eat his vegetables. I have flipped the script because I simply understand and accept the truth of that tired and overused cliché that my parents ran in the ground, "Vegetables may not be good to you, but they are good for you." Because I Love Bryce, in order to take care of him, I must occasionally make him do things he doesn't want to do.

Interestingly enough, this aspect of what it means to take care of someone is often lost on me when it comes to taking care of myself. When adults talk about taking care of ourselves, our minds go to our need to take a vacation, get some rest, or make time to be pampered. True, many of us could use some time to do these things, but I am realizing that there is an aspect of taking care of ourselves that we often miss. Just as I must make my son eat his literal vegetables while taking care of him, I must make myself eat my metaphorical vegetables to take care of myself. No, I am not talking about broccoli, asparagus, or brussels sprouts, though I could probably use some catching up on those as well. I am talking about doing those things that are not good to me, but are good for me. In this sense, plenty of us are guilty of not eating our vegetables.

When we don't eat our vegetables, we suffer from malnutrition. Our bodies suffer, our dreams wilt, and a gap widens between what we can be and what we are.

RIGHT NOW, SO MANY OF US ARE NOT TAKING CARE OF OURSELVES BECAUSE WE ARE NOT WILLING TO PRESS THROUGH AND DO THE THINGS IN LIFE THAT DON'T FEEL GOOD TO US, BUT MAKE ALL THE DIFFERENCE IN OUR GROWTH, PROGRESS, AND SUCCESS.

So many of us won't work the extra hours, stop eating the unhealthy foods, let go of the toxic relationships, skip some of the night life, make ourselves do the exercise, cut down on our spending, or commit to our intentional spiritual development because to do so doesn't feel good. In other words, we are not taking care of ourselves. The difference in where we are, where we want to be, and where God would have us to be, is lying in our ability to sacrifice what tastes good, feels good, and sounds good for what will actually be good for our life. So, I pray that we can begin to Love ourselves enough to suck it up, hold our nose, close our eyes, take a deep breath, and eat our vegetables.

58
3 Questions Every Christian Should Ask About Their Position on Same-Sex Marriage

This past Sunday I offered the congregation that I pastor three questions that I thought would be helpful as they get their mind around their position on the legalization of Same-Sex Marriage. These three questions are by no means exhaustive, but I do think they are beneficial to those who call themselves followers of Jesus. It was not my goal to demand they take one position or another, but it was my goal to give them tools that might help them think thoroughly and theologically about this issue. Below, are the three questions I offered.

First, *do I hold my position Lovingly?* As Christians, I maintain that our most important creed, highest standard, and most sacred ambition should be to Love. What has been saddest to me in this latest surge in discussion over same-sex marriage, is how un-Lovingly people who follow Jesus have been. There has not only been a lack of Love in the expressions and sentiments given, but more importantly Love has not been a factor in the rationalizations, thought processes, and considerations that help form these expressions and sentiments in the first place. Many seem not to ask or concern themselves with the question, "What would Love have me do in this situation?" How much should Love push me to allow someone the right to disagree with me and to live in their position? Does Love ask me to consider what it feels like to be in the shoes of another? The question of Love is relevant to both sides of the debate, but as always, I believe the burden to live in Love always weighs more heavily on those with power, privilege, and position.

Second, *do I hold my position consistently?* The church, particularly the African-American Church, has not openly discussed and debated the topic of legalizing same-sex marriage enough. Therefore, like most ideas, when there is not a lot of talk, there is not a lot of thought. Democratic discussion leads to depth, and many of us have positions with no intellectual depth or theological consistency. I have heard over and over Biblical appeals to the "Word of God," as reasons why same-sex marriage should not be legal. Yet, most people who hold this view do not understand what they are asking and hold this view in direct contradiction to other views they hold. An example of this is clearly seen when we compare our view about God and Jesus to marriage. The Bible clearly states that "you shall have no other God before me (Exodus 20:3)." Yet, most Christians champion the cause of freedom of religion in the United States and are extremely proud of this right our country upholds. Sit with that for a minute. Most American Christians hold sacred the right to be or not be Christian. We believe people should have the right to disagree with us on God and live in their beliefs. We believe they should have the right to be Hindu, Buddhist, agnostic and/or atheist. In spite of the scriptures that deal with the divinity and uniqueness of Jesus, we believe that Americans should have the right to believe that Jesus is God, a prophet, a great man, or just a fairy tale. In other words, we do not use the bible as the standard to set laws about how people approach God or Jesus. The question of consistency begs us to ask, why we would do such about marriage. Consistency asks us to explain why we are willing to live and let live on God and Jesus, but we are not willing to do this with marriage. How is it that we can give up legislating the most central part of Christianity (i.e. CHRIST), but feel the need for national laws to uphold what many Christians believe about marriage? We must also ask, "If my position is inconsistent, what is motivating my inconsistency?"

WHY IS IT THAT I CAN SUPPORT TROOPS DYING FOR THE RIGHT FOR EVERYONE TO CHOOSE THEIR OWN GOD (OR TO CHOOSE NO GOD AT ALL), BUT I WOULD RATHER DIE THAN GIVE PEOPLE THE RIGHT TO CHOOSE THEIR OWN LIFE PARTNER?

There is not only inconsistency in choosing when to use the bible as a reason for legislature, but we are also inconsistent in choosing when the bible should be the guide for our actions and the actions we celebrate. The bible clearly supports obeying the governing authorities (Romans 13:1) and even goes so far as to demand slaves to obey their masters (Colossians 3:22). This biblical call to obey the government does not make an exception for sit-ins, protests, and any other boycotts of the law. However, every time we celebrate the civil rights movement we applaud civil and at least in part biblical disobedience. As much as I Love Harriet Tubman and the Underground Railroad, there is nothing biblically based about stealing the property that slave owners had a legal right to own. The bible does not support breaking the laws of the government in this way. Many Christians of the 21st Century not only ignore this, but in the case of freedom fighters, civil rights activists, and abolitionists, we applaud this. How is it that we are comfortable ignoring the bible (at least parts of it) in these cases? Where is the consistency in our use of the bible? And even though I find it nearly impossible to follow every single biblical injunction, I do think one should take the time to at least THINK about why we choose some parts over others—particularly, when we use some of those parts to say people should not have rights.

Finally, *do I hold my position relatively?* This question asks us to consider the fact that no position stands in a vacuum. I have heard too many people use the issue of same gender Love as the tipping point that determines their support of a person, place, or even a church. We must always ask ourselves about the relationship and value any of our commitments have to each other. How do we hold one position in relation to others? It saddens me at times to hear anyone reduce their political or personal affiliation to one issue. In a country that is in conflict on the responsibility of the richest people in our society, health care, the prison industry, unemployment and underemployment, racial profiling, foreign policy, and a host of other issues, to lend or withdraw our support over emotional reactions to one issue seems deeply irresponsible. As we search and struggle for a socially healthy community and country, we must strive for political progress that searches for Loving, just, and equitable treatment in every arena of our lives.

Do I hold my position Lovingly? Do I hold my position consistently? Do I hold my position relatively? These questions do not tell us what to think, but hopefully they help guide us on a few things to think about. In dealing with an issue that touches people at the depths of their existence, we owe it to ourselves and to our neighbors to think deeply, reflect diligently, and discuss democratically. Most importantly, however, as Christians we owe it to God, others, and ourselves to Love unconditionally.

59
Humility

Humility is one of the most overused and misused words in our everyday discourse. Often we label anyone who is shy, soft-spoken, or insecure – humble. Even less compatible with humility are low self-esteem, low self-image, and low self-worth. Cornel West, in his book Restoring Hope, commented on humility in a conversation with historian James Melvin Washington and pastor James Forbes when he asserted, "You can't have humility without confidence and security. If you're insecure, you're not going to be humble. In fact, it might make you sadomasochistic." Though I knew he was onto something by connecting confidence with humility, it was difficult for me to wrap my mind around exactly what he meant.

As I was working on a sermon a few weeks ago, I was reading and re-reading a passage in Philippians chapter two. In the fifth through eighth verse it says, "Let the same mind be in you that was in Christ Jesus, who, though he was in the form of God, did not regard equality with God as something to be exploited, but emptied himself … and became obedient to the point of death." Though this text is so rich with theological possibility and so eligible for theological disagreement, I believe that it provides a great road map to understanding the relationship between confidence and humility. The reason West argues that you are not going to be humble if you are insecure is because humility is a choice to not allow what is best and brightest in us and about us to consume our relationship to the world. However, if insecurity and low self-esteem destroy our ability to cherish the good in us, we can never make the choice to be humble.

HUMILITY DOES NOT DENY MY PERSONAL GREATNESS, BUT IT IS ALSO NOT CONSUMED BY IT.

In the midst of greatness, humility reminds us that we are still created to make a contribution to the world through service. In this passage, Jesus has every reason to make the world about him (he was made in the form of God), yet humility drives Jesus to exist for the world.

On one hand, being engrossed with ourselves makes it extremely difficult to submit ourselves to the kind of service that gives a contribution to the world. On the other hand, without the confidence and the security that God has equipped us with, we will not substantially impact our environment for the better. If we Love ourselves too much the world won't matter enough for us to want to improve it. If we Love ourselves too little we won't matter enough for us to believe we can improve it. So I want to challenge those of us who have been giving false credit to others and ourselves for being shy, soft spoken, and insecure. I also want to contest those of us who have been giving ourselves too much credit by assuming the world revolves around us. Most of all, I want to encourage someone to make the choice of humility, not because you have to, but because the world needs you to. Ahhh, so there we have it – I have achieved humility when I realize the world needs me, while never allowing myself to think the world is about me.

60
Faith

We have all heard that fear is the greatest obstacle to faith. However, I learned something more about both some time ago at my son's swim lesson. Bryce had his first swim lesson at six months old. We would get in the water together, I would hold him, and we would do different exercises together. Each lesson would amaze me as I watched Bryce's increasing comfort in the water because of his unyielding faith in the security of being in my arms. By the time he was one year old, he was comfortable going under the water and coming back up without crying. Then, the swim lessons stopped and they did not resume until Bryce was three years old. It was the same pool, it was the same water, but there was a different little boy. In that period of time between swim lessons, Bryce gained a fear of the water.

At one of Bryce's last swim lessons I was amused as Bryce adjusted the instructions of the teacher to fit his fears of the water. First, the teacher told him to grab a flotation device, stretch his arms out, lay flat and kick. Instead of stretching his arms out and grabbing the device, he brought the device to his chest, placed the device under his arms, and made sure it was securely under him so that he would not go under the water. Then, instead of laying horizontal in the water and kicking, Bryce decided that he would be more secure if he stood up vertically in the water and kicked. All of a sudden Bryce's teacher starts laughing because Bryce is kicking frantically, but going nowhere.

It was at this point that my sermonic antennae went up and my theological telescope began to focus. Bryce's fear of the water, lack of faith in the buoyancy of the device his teacher had given him, and lack of faith in the instructions his teacher had told him translated into Bryce doing his own thing - kicking as hard as he could but not going anywhere. In some sense, many of us are like Bryce in the waters of life. We are kicking, maybe even pedaling and swinging our arms, but we are going nowhere and not making any progress. My child needed to have faith that what his teacher had given him would hold him up. He needed to believe if he did what the teacher said, he would get back to the bank of the pool. But he did not believe and as a result he was in the middle of the water going nowhere. As children of God, we often lack the faith that God has equipped us with what we need to keep us afloat in life, and God has instructions for our lives that if we would just follow, we could get somewhere. Still we know what Bryce intuitively knew in that swim class—that faith, just like laying horizontally in the water, means putting ourselves in a vulnerable position. Nevertheless, it sometimes takes being vulnerable to make progress. It may take the vulnerability of trust in a relationship; the vulnerability of following our calling no matter what; the vulnerability of listening to our spirit when it opposes conventionality and popular opinion.

What Bryce taught me in that swimming pool was simply this:

FAITH IS NOT JUST SOMETHING WE NEED TO BE PLEASING TO GOD, IT IS ALSO SOMETHING WE NEED TO MAKE PROGRESS FOR OURSELVES.

Faith places us in the posture and position that will move us the furthest and the fastest.

61

"The Extra Mile"

Am I the only one who has trouble getting excited about the "turn the other cheek" passages? In three short verses in Matthew 5, Jesus gives most of us a bit more than we can chew. First, he invites us to turn the other cheek when hit, then he suggests that if we are sued for our coat we should give up our sweater also and just avoid the hassle. Then, as if the former is not already enough, he asks us to go a second mile when forced to go one mile. For years I have heard people give reason after reason as to why this passage does not apply to them. I have been one of those people. Recently, however, I have seen these prescriptions in a new light.

The source of light that has changed my view about Jesus' "extra mile" instructions came when I read about the former leader of Ritz-Carlton Hotels and current founder and CEO of West Paces Hotel Group – Horst Schulze. Under his leadership, Ritz-Carlton has become a premier-brand amongst hotel chains. It has developed loyal customers who refuse to stay elsewhere when a Ritz-Carlton hotel is in town. Schulze did this, in part, by taking customer service to unprecedented levels. Staff was encouraged to learn names, find out the personal tastes of hotel guests, and make them feel treasured. When most hotels were finding new ways to stack up charges, raise prices, and increase profits, Horst Schulze was challenging Ritz-Carlton employees to go above and beyond to make guests feel served. As I was reflecting on the genius and efficacy of Schulze, I began to realize that his career was in large part built on asking people to go the extra mile.

Soon it began to dawn on me that all this time I had been missing the brilliance of what Jesus was saying in the Sermon on the Mount. By reducing Jesus' exhortations to the particularities of the examples and not seeing it as a principle to live by, I blinded myself to all the benefits of the principle of the extra mile. Schulze saw the benefits of going the extra mile in business and led a prestigious hotel into preeminence. Google saw the benefit of going the extra mile to make their employees comfortable and has become a world leading company where people crave to be employed. Countless athletes have ascended to Hall of Fame careers because they went the extra mile in their practice routines and off-season preparations. In fact, in what realm of life does going the extra mile not pay tremendous benefits?

Maybe Jesus knew that if we could go the extra mile for those who didn't deserve it, then going beyond the call of duty for everyone else would be easy. Maybe he was trying to inject us with a principle that helps our careers, our businesses, our dreams, and our spirit.

MAYBE HE UNDERSTOOD, UNLIKE US, THAT GOING ABOVE AND BEYOND IS NEVER ABOUT THE OTHER PERSON BUT IT IS ABOUT US. MAYBE HE UNDERSTOOD THAT JUST LIKE SERVING PEOPLE EXTRAVAGANTLY MAKES BETTER COMPANIES, LOVING PEOPLE EXCESSIVELY MAKES BETTER PEOPLE.

Making the extra mile particular to enemies is frustrating, however making it a universal principle to live by is liberating. So, go find the border of responsibility and cross it, the barrier of just enough and shatter it, the line where you don't have to give anymore and go beyond it. For there are benefits and blessings at the end of the extra mile.

62
The Extra Thought

In my previous reflection I extolled the virtues of Jesus' going the extra mile passages. I talked about it as a principle that has ameliorative and rewarding benefits in our lives. However, I was challenged by two ladies who troubled the possible implications of my conclusions and Jesus' statements about the extra mile. One was a sister I have recently become acquainted with, and the other was a long-time friend, scholar and activist. Both of them are from different parts of the world, with different backgrounds, but with the same critical question. "How does the 'extra mile' concept affect women who are suffering from the oppression of male chauvinism, supremacy, and patriarchy?" Put in more general terms, "If one has been culturally and socially trained to live with an inferiority complex that calls for one to constantly reduce oneself for the benefit of another, wouldn't the extra mile concept give Divine sanction to an unhealthy prioritization of others?" In essence, for those who are oppressed, the extra mile concept can actually become a hindrance to self-Love. If I find myself going above and beyond for someone I have been made to believe is more valuable than me, I never know if my extra is a result of a lesser view of myself and an unfounded greater view of another. Thus, going the extra mile can simply be a perpetuation of an inferiority complex.

I readily admit there are problems with the idea of going the "extra mile." It can fuel an inferiority complex, deepen low self-esteem, and further entrench us in an oppressive relationship if not judiciously applied in our living. To be sure, every relationship we are in and every encounter we have is not one marked by oppression. As tricky as this concept can be for women in relation to men, it may be just as helpful in women's relationships with each other. As much as it may be harmful for black men in the context of white supremacy, there are countless other places where it may be helpful. There are simply places in our lives where going above and beyond is "a principle that helps our careers, our businesses, our dreams and even our spirit." Ultimately, I do believe there are places in most women's lives where going above and beyond is enriching to their lives and rewarding to a given relationship.

Oppressive relationships are not such a place. This is the problem with "The Extra Mile," that I did not voice and that makes a simple proclamation about the value of the extra mile provincial. Oppression needs some concept of inferiority and servitude to exist healthily. I did not point out, and I should have, how Jesus' turn the other cheek sentiments, go the extra mile thoughts, and even death on the cross is used to ask women and other oppressed people to suffer through oppression, endure inequity, and bear physical, psychological, and emotional abuse. These are the times I wish I could put Jesus on the cross examination stand and ask him how he balances his call to go the extra mile with his demand for us to Love ourselves as children of God. When is going the extra mile harmful to our very being and self-esteem, and when is it rewarding and enriching to our spirit? We cannot put Jesus on the witness stand. Yet, we can put his followers on the witness stand, and this is what my two sisters did to me. The truth is I can give no absolute answer as to when one should go the extra mile and when one should take a stand for justice and self. I can say we should do both! I can also say that Jesus places the greatest priority on us Loving our neighbor as ourselves.

THIS MEANS WE CANNOT LOVE OURSELVES LESS THAN OUR NEIGHBOR, LESS WE BE OPPRESSED. YET, WE CANNOT LOVE OURSELVES MORE THAN OUR NEIGHBOR, LESS WE BE NARCISSISTS.

Love Better

We CAN Love our neighbor as ourselves and allow Love to be the determining factor in all that we do.

63
Who Do You Love?

In October of 2015 many of us were witnesses to a video of a white police officer from South Carolina body slamming a teenage black girl and dragging her across the floor because she was not doing what was asked of her by her teacher. For me, incidents like this offers extreme experiences that test our loyalty and our Love. To my dismay, there were those who acknowledged the wrong of the officer, but spent the weight of their efforts, energies, and exhortations criticizing the child, bemoaning modern youth, and lamenting present day parenting. Others, seemed to not even acknowledge that the officer was wrong, but were caught up in the game of "she started it" by pointing to her original defiance as the "real" problem.

Adults all around the world had an opportunity to prove their Love and loyalty to children. Unfortunately, too many held up the age-old age-ist standard whereby appropriate adult behavior must be precipitated by flawless actions by our children. The only rationale I can muster for this is the argument for chronology. Essentially, since her wrong was first, it must be the wrong prioritized. A lot of people are fooled by this narrow minded and short-sighted way of thinking. Who was wrong "first" is but one standard of judgment. Who had the greater responsibility is another.

On one hand, we had a young child our society has deemed too young and immature to vote, too young and immature to fight for our country, and too young and immature to drink a wine cooler. We had a child who was still a student yet to finish the basic education system our country has deemed necessary and foundational to being a responsible adult. Yet, this same child who, by almost every public measure, should not be held to an adult standard somehow bore the weight of the responsibility in the violence she endured.

On the other hand, we had a grown man who has been deemed old enough to vote, fight for our country, and drink alcohol. He has completed his basic education, been trained and certified to have his job, and is paid by public dollars and trusted by the same public to serve his community and act appropriately with and for its citizens. This grown man signed a contract committing him to appropriate behavior. So, when this child and grown man get into a confrontation and both are wrong, it seems ridiculous to resort to the kindergarten argument of, "Yeah, but she started it." Making the insubordination of a child equal to the brutality of an adult is what is called a false equivalency. Non-violent defiance by a girl does not deserve violent persecution by a man.

Yet, somehow there was a familiar voice in our society, blacks and whites included, that abandoned support of a child in favor of a man. Moreover, once again the actions of a young black girl were decried while a grown white man was defended. The innocence of her childhood seemed to go out the window as many rallied around age, whiteness, and maleness and chose to castigate a young black girl, rather than publicly criticize and condemn a grown white man. This was an opportunity for us to prove that young black female lives do matter enough for us to stand up and defend them. Some did. Many did.

HOWEVER, FAR TOO MANY INSIDE AND OUTSIDE OF THE BLACK COMMUNITY SEEMED TO ONCE AGAIN SUGGEST THAT BLACK PEOPLE HAVE TO BE PERFECT IN ORDER FOR US TO DEMAND THAT WHITE PEOPLE BE JUST. OUR BLACK GIRLS DESERVE MORE THAN THAT.

They deserve more of our Love and more of our loyalty even when they are wrong. To be clear standing up for black children when they are wrong is NOT to condone their behavior. It is, however, to affirm their humanity. And in the end, a child not leaving a room when asked does not give an adult a pass to brutalize her.

Jesus was once put in an extreme experience that tested his Love and loyalty. A group of religious people caught a woman in the wrong of adultery and wanted to exact deadly violence, while somehow the condemnation of the man was nowhere to be found (John 8:1-11). There was no doubt she was guilty, and there was even less doubt that a very sexist law said kill her. In a moment where Jesus could have chosen tradition, punishment, principle, or the prioritization of a woman's perfection – Jesus chose compassion, forgiveness, and understanding. In fact, throughout the gospels, Jesus offers us a paradigm for how to extend our loyalties and our Love. He suggests that we side with the vulnerable, the weak, the least, the lost, and the last in our world. Over and over again Jesus prioritizes who many in society minimize. In a moment where a young black girl was manhandled, Christians all over the nation had a chance to choose Jesus, and people all over the nation had a chance to choose the life of a young black girl. Many did. Too many did not. The legacy of our country is one that has taught and continues to teach us to de-prioritize the humanity of black people, young people and women. Sadly, we were again reminded that others don't Love us and we don't Love ourselves …. enough.

64
Another Level

Hannah Kinoti tells a true story about an African shepherd boy named Semoine who was twelve years old when he had his first confrontation with a lion. He, along with five other boys, was grazing a herd of cows in the Maasai Mara game reserve when, surprised by a lion, the other boys ran away and left Semoine alone to face the vicious beast of prey. As the lion was creeping upon a cow that Semoine had just milked that morning, he threw his spear and struck the lion in the chest. All of a sudden the wounded beast attacked the boy, breaking his right leg and then mauling his head. Semoine spent two months in the hospital but still declared he would challenge any lion again if it attacked his daddy's herd. THAT is another level!

We often hear, quote, and read the 23rd Psalm, but never has it been more alive for me than when I read this story. This story invites us to imagine the shepherd metaphor for God with a whole new meaning, life, and vitality. It paints a picture of a God who is vigilant about out safety and security and will risk everything for our life. The story of Semoine helps us merge the metaphor of shepherd with the reality of the cross. Here is God using Jesus to step in front of us and risk it all so that we might have life more abundantly, walk more freely, exist more justly, and love more heartily. Can't you hear that young African boy, with a cast on his leg and bandages all about his skull, vociferously declaring, "Yeah, I did it, and I'll do it again if a lion attacks one of my Daddy's cows." More than this, I hear Jesus, with blood dripping, hands throbbing, feet hurting, and head aching, saying, "This is what I do when lions attack my daddy's children." THAT is another level!

Yet, the question is: are we willing to go to another level? Interestingly enough we do not go to another level by basking in the glory of God's shepherd like qualities. Yes, God is worthy of our awe, praise, and worship, but we don't take it to another level by going to church more, yelling louder, dancing more feverishly, or "praising" more fervently. It is easy to be a sheep who are excited about how we are given protection, peace, and provisions from the Good Shepherd. The challenge for us is to not just applaud the efforts of our Shepherd, but rather to accept the invitation to be shepherds ourselves. This invitation is given to all who will take seriously the idea that we are created in God's image. God's gift to us is protect us as sheep. God's call to us is to help protect other sheep.

WE ARE CALLED TO DO MORE THAN SIMPLY ACCEPT GOD'S LOVE. WE ARE CALLED TO EMBODY IT.

With all the gifts, talents, and blessings we have been bestowed with, are we running away or sitting idly by while God's children are being attacked by lions? Who will get up and risk life and limb for someone or someone's ability to flower and flourish in an enemy stricken pasture? Moreover, after we've been injured in battle and hurt by the enemy, who will declare while the bandages are still on and the wounds are still festering that I will continue to fight if lions attack God's children? THAT is another level!

65

Love Makes Room

Parenting teaches you so much about yourself. There is so much Love, ability, and energy that I did not know I had until becoming a father. The other day I was unpacking my SUV to get ready to go home, and as usual it felt like I was moving back in my apartment. Backpack, extra bag for books, grocery bags, hairbrush, and CD was just some of the stuff I was unloading. A friend of mine looked in amazement while seeming to be entertained as I used my shoulders, forearms, hands, and hips to try to hold everything together. Just as I had finished my balancing act and was ready to begin my baggage filled trip to my front door, my two-year old son looks at me and demands that I pick him up.

I am convinced that toddlers are born with a magical ability to discern the absolute most inconvenient time to ask for something and then proceed to make demands. Here I was, literally covered with bags, and Bryce has now decided that there is no possible way that he can walk by himself to the front door. At this point my friend perceives my dilemma and offers to help by asking to take something off of my hands. Surprisingly, I declined because I have managed to find a way to pick Bryce up no matter how much other stuff I am holding in and on my arms. So, I responded in a humorously arrogant way, "I am a Father, I've learned how to pick up Bryce when my hands are full."

Whether it is because I am a first-time parent or I am simply soft-hearted, I have trouble saying no to Bryce when he wants to be picked up. Even when it seems that I am swamped with stuff on my shoulders, forearms, hands, and hips, I can always manage to make just enough room for Bryce. I believe that there is something about Love that makes a way. There is something about Love that always makes room.

I want to assure you today that we serve a God whose Love always makes room for us.

DESPITE THE PERPETUAL PROBLEMS OF THE WORLD AND THE POLYPHONY OF PRAYERS GOD HEARS, GOD'S HEART ALWAYS HAS ROOM FOR MY HEARTACHES.

When I cry, God always clears a finger to wipe my tears. When I call, God always clears a phone line to accept my ring. And when I need to be held, God always makes some room to pick me up. We have a Father, whose Love can hold us even when God's hands are full.

66
Home Court Advantage

If you have ever played, observed, or been at a sporting event, then you know what it means for a player or a team to have the "home court advantage." This idea refers to the reality that most teams play better and win more when they are at a venue where the audience is cheering for them and supporting their efforts. Yet, have you ever really thought about how powerful the "home court advantage" actually is and what constitutes this power?

Spectators go to a game and shout frantically, cheer feverishly, and even jump, point, and shake their fists frenetically in an attempt to literally will their team into victory. Interestingly enough, nothing they do actually gives any physical assistance to players. They cannot give anyone a better aim, make anyone stronger, or provide anyone more speed, athleticism, or quickness. However, all the statistics tell us that an overwhelming amount of teams win more games at home than they do on the road. Cheering does not give a team a better strategy, nor does it provide a tactical advantage. Yet time and time again players perform better and teams are more victorious when they are at home receiving encouragement and support from people who are on their side and want them to win. The amazing key to the home court advantage is while it is not a physical, strategic, or tactical advantage, it is a spiritual advantage. There is something about the cheers of the crowd, the energy that it forms in the arena, and the inspiration that it provides for the players that make them more likely to win. The advantage given to the players is not touched or seen, it is felt! In essence, the home court advantage is a testament to the power of COMMUNITY.

As we go through life and face obstacles and opponents, both seen and unseen, it is extremely important for us to recognize the value of creating our own "home court advantage." Our chances of winning the varying and voluminous battles of life get much better, when we have people cheering for our success, pushing for us to play better, and hoping that we will win. Therefore, winning in life takes more than just attending to our own individual needs and personal preparation.

IT BENEFITS OUR CAUSE AND BEHOOVES OUR LIFE TO FIND AND FORM COMMUNITIES THAT WILL NURTURE, SUSTAIN, CARE, AND LOVE US.

For all of its faults, this is the value of church! Church should at least provide you a community that is praying, preaching, and pulling for your triumph. We need people in the bleachers of and around our lives screaming frantically, cheering feverishly, and gesturing frenetically to the end that we score a point, make a basket, and win the game. Community gives us a better chance at victory! The "home court advantage" helps us win.

Who gives you your "home court advantage?" As you fast, pray, read self-help books, practice, and work towards developing yourself and your spirituality, don't make your journey insular and individualistic. Pay careful attention to the people in and around your life and make sure they are cheering and not booing, pulling for your success and not rooting for you failure. If you find yourself playing life's game on the road, then let me encourage you today to find people who want you to win and go home.

B.A. Jackson is the Lead Pastor of Fellowship of Love Church in Fayetteville, GA (a suburb of Atlanta). Organized in 2008, it has become one of the fastest growing progressive Christian churches in the area. The vision of Fellowship of Love is to revolutionize the idea and the impact of church. In just 10 years, this ministry has restored many people's faith in the efficacy and relevance of the church, helped people believe and be baptized, renewed spiritual lives, created music to inspire the world, and given almost $500,000 to over two dozen organizations, schools, and groups of people. If you are ever in the area, please come by and worship with them.

www.bajackson.com
www.fellowshipoflovechurch.org

B.A. Jackson is available for lectures, "book talks," and speaking engagements. To inquire about the possibility of having him appear at your next event, please email ba@bajackson.com.